Comments about

The Art of Taking Action: Lessons from Japanese Psychology

*The **Art of Taking Action** is an elegant approach to helping individuals deal with the dysfunctional relationships that lay at the root of many psychiatric problems. It offers a concise and practical approach to facilitating compassionate living even in the depths of despair.*

- Robert Strayhan, M.D.

***The Art of Taking Action** is a door way into living a life of accomplishment and satisfaction that leaves no one out. A cookbook for life -- providing guidance and recipes that will nourish you and those around you. It addresses the kinds of challenges we all face in cooking our life, and is the best book of its kind that I've ever encountered.*

- Ron Hogen Green, Zen teacher, MRO

*In **The Art of Taking Action**, Gregg Krech has created a set of cables for jump starting projects of any size. And once the project is on the road, Krech uses wit and timeless spiritual wisdom to provide a map for the entire journey.*

- Victoria Register-Freeman, author, Love Stories from the Bible

The Art of Taking Action *is a cry for us to leave analysis and theory behind, and actually engage with what needs to be done in our lives. These principles have certainly been important in my own life and in the lives of my patients. I highly recommend this text to all.*

- Henry McCann, Doctor of Acupuncture and Oriental Medicine

The Art of Taking Action:

Lessons from Japanese Psychology

By Gregg Krech

Assistant Editor

Nancie S. Martin

Contributors

Trudy Boyle

Linda Anderson Krech

Jennifer Bucko Lamplough

Kate Manahan

Margaret McKenzie

Donella Meadows

Susan Page

Stephen Pressfield

Sharon Salzberg

Shinichi Suzuki

Jarno Virtanen

The Art

of

Taking

Action:

Lessons from

Japanese

Psychology

By Gregg Krech

Published by the ToDo Institute

A 501(c)(3) not for profit organization

PO Box 50

Monkton, VT 05469
(802) 453-4440

www.todoinstitute.org

www.todoinstitutebooks.com

www.thirtythousanddays.org

The publisher would like to gratefully acknowledge those individuals who gave permission for their writing to appear in this book. Thank you.

Cover design: by Amanda Coyle. Cover image photo by Yasunari Nakamura.

Some of the material in this book previously appeared in *Thirty Thousand Days: A Journal of Purposeful Living*, a publication of the ToDo Institute. Used by permission. All rights reserved. Some of the essays from this book were originally published in *A Concise Little Guide to Getting Things Done*, also a publication of the ToDo Institute.

Dedicated to my father

Ted A. Krech (1927-2014)

During my childhood my father would leave for work each morning between midnight and 1AM. He worked for a wholesale bakery in Chicago. He arrived at the bakery, loaded a 21 foot truck with more than 1,000 lbs. of bakery goods and then drove around the city delivering bread, bagels and dinner rolls to supermarkets, delis and restaurants. 1,000 lbs. on – 1,000 lbs. off. He did this six days per week for more than forty years. For some of those years he worked a second job on Sundays to earn additional money for our family. He was, and still is, my personal model of effort and hard work. Thank you, Dad.

Is This Book for You?

There is a Buddhist story about four kinds of horses. The first horse is the best horse. He is responsive to the driver's will without even seeing the shadow of the whip. The second best horse will respond quickly to the sound of the driver's voice or, as soon as he sees the shadow of the whip. The third horse will run when he feels pain from the touch of the whip against his skin. And the fourth horse won't move until he feels the pain from the whip penetrate to the marrow of his bones. When it comes to taking action, which type of horse are you?

Realistically, you're probably a different horse in different situations. You may be an excellent horse when it comes to washing your dinner dishes, and you may be a horse that avoids writing, at any cost, the novel that's in your head. But most of us wish we were the excellent horse, no matter what situation we are faced with. Not only do we want to take the right action at the right time, but we want to do it mindfully, gratefully, competently and without being distracted.

Before you read any further, I'd like to clearly state that if you function like the first horse, even most of the time, this book will offer you little benefit. You'll pick up a few tips and probably enjoy the ideas, but if you're already at the top of your game, then I offer you my sincere respect and admiration.

This book is written more for the other three horses and particularly for the last two who are in pain. Most of the time it takes pain to get them to move. Can you relate to that? If so, then this book can offer you something different. It's not just about doing more and procrastinating less. It's about your dreams, your passion, the risks you need to take and the opportunity to forget yourself and simply disappear into the moment as it unfolds. It's about less talk and more action. It's about less blaming and more appreciation. It's about less mindlessness and more presence.

So now you may be thinking that this book will help you become one of the "best horses." Well . . . not necessarily. Here's the paradox: it's the fourth horse, the one who feels the most pain, who has the truest spirit. It's the fourth horse who has the biggest heart. The fourth horse has very little pride and arrogance and also has the most compassion for other horses who are struggling, because struggle is the thread of that horse's daily existence.

You don't need to become the best horse or even the second best horse (after all, you're not really a horse at all). You just need to figure out how to work with your life – with your circumstances, your feelings, your family members, your challenges, your dreams and your disappointments. You have to figure out what you need to do, when you need to do it, and how to do it to the best of your ability. There's nobody whipping you from behind. Your life is in front of you, waiting . . . for your next move.

"Everyday life is like an inexpressibly fascinating new movie, which can't be guessed at ahead of time. In it I find myself dancing, crying, laughing, shouting, singing, suffering, enjoying. And from the inner core, all this fans the flames of hope still larger. My hope is neither the result of expectation nor the expectation of results. The way of hope is that of great nature itself, transcending cause and effect. Hope itself is light and life. Listen to this hope speaking from out of my soul: 'Come now, with intense and honest mind. I will protect you. Do not fear the descent into fire and water. Do not fear any evil.' Let's advance, shattering all difficulties. Let's go onward, following the way of hope!"

- Haya Akegarasu

TABLE OF CONTENTS

The Art of Taking Action

Preface

Many of us associate Eastern philosophy and religion with contemplative practices, such as meditation (zazen) or self-reflection (Naikan). We've borrowed from the contemplative East in order to integrate practices such as yoga, mindfulness or calligraphy into our lives. But there is also a foundation of Eastern wisdom directed towards ACTION. We tend to overlook these ideas because we may see our lives as already too active – too much to do and not enough time to do it. But the action principles that come from the East are different from those in the West. They emphasize a value system grounded in principles such as non-attachment, purpose, gratitude, interdependence, and coexisting with fear. Such principles are prominent in martial arts (Aikido, Kyudo), psychology (Morita therapy, Kaizen) and even religion (engaged Buddhism). The *Art of Taking Action* isn't simply about keeping busy or checking things off your to-do list. It's about choosing what to do, how to do it, and the development of character.

No person more elegantly manifests the art of taking action more than Mahatma Gandhi. As the grandfather of the non-violence movement, Gandhi inspired millions to consider non-violent resistance as a method of civil disobedience and change. On the surface, we might see his methods as an excellent example of inaction. You do not run. You do not fight. You do not resist. You do not cooperate. And yet, his philosophy created a revolution against one of the greatest colonial powers of modern times – England. Gandhi, himself, was a man of strong willpower and action. He never preached passivity or withdrawal from the world of human affairs. The meditation teacher Eknath Easwaran described Gandhi's character this way:

"Very, very few people in human history have accomplished more than Gandhi. Not many people even have the colossal vitality he had. But he generally looked so relaxed that a superficial observer might have thought he was lazy. If you look at some of the pictures of Gandhi, he looks so relaxed that he reminds me of our cat. . . Actually, although Gandhi looks frail in photographs, he had not only a Ferrari engine but a Ferrari body as well. Only a strong, resilient body could have taken the rigors of that life. John Gunther, who was over six feet tall, recalled that he had to run to keep up with Gandhi when he went to interview him, and Gandhi was in his seventies at the time. His vigor was unmistakable. His power was untouched until the

situation demanded it; then he would take off in no time, from zero to sixty in one minute, as calm as ever behind the wheel. It was all power steering too, just the opposite of the stereotype of the tense, time-driven man of action. I was only a student when I met him, and it gave me a whole new idea of what it means to operate successfully in the modern world."

Many of Gandhi's biographers confirm his reputation as a man of action. But they also describe him as a man of spirituality and prayer. Though he is best remembered for his leadership of non-violent resistance which ultimately liberated India from colonial authority, he also demonstrated how we can integrate both contemplative practice and action.

A Stack of Dirty Dishes

About 30 years after Gandhi's death, I moved into a freshly painted one-bedroom apartment in Alexandria, Virginia. I was twenty-two years old and ready to take on the world. It was my first "solo" experience – no roommates, no dog, no parents, no siblings. I could leave my dirty socks on the dining room table and stay up late playing my guitar. I reveled in the freedom of my solitude and space.

About three weeks later, I was making myself dinner when I realized that I was completely out of dishes – all the plates and bowls were piled in the sink and had been waiting patiently, for quite some time, to be washed. So I did what any self-respecting young bachelor would do. *I raced over to the convenience store to buy paper plates.* Why those dishes hadn't been washed is a bit mysterious, given the well-functioning dishwasher that occupied a small space under the counter not far from the sink. I never did figure out how to get the dishwasher to reach over, grab the dishes, turn itself on and stack the plates neatly in the overhead cabinet. My role in the process, while essential, was limited. It didn't require great strength or intelligence. The task was not particularly complex. The time required was minimal. Yet I was passive – a man of inaction. What kept me from taking action – from doing what needed to be done?

It wasn't just washing dishes that I avoided. It included work deadlines, tax returns, paying bills, returning library books and just about anything else that needed to be done, but didn't stimulate positive feelings.

Ten years later I discovered the work of a Japanese psychiatrist that provided more than just insight into my struggles with procrastination. His work offered me a set of practical strategies for moving forward and taking action even when I didn't feel like it.

Shoma Morita, M.D. (1874-1938) developed a model of psychology now known as Morita Therapy. Rooted in Zen and borrowing ideas from an Eastern worldview, it is a stark contrast to the European-based mental health models we have become familiar with. Not long after Morita Therapy was developed, a Japanese man named Ishin Yoshimoto (1916 -1988) developed a profound, yet practical, method of self-reflection. Yoshimoto came from the contemplative side of Buddhism and developed an approach called Naikan (*inside looking*), which emphasized personal transformation through self-examination and self-awareness.

As a student of Buddhism, I was attracted to these two approaches, and have now studied and taught "Japanese Psychology" for the past 28 years. In this book I'll share with you some of the principles, ideas and strategies that have helped me personally and have been applied by those who have studied with me at the ToDo Institute during this time.

I call this book *The Art of Taking Action*, because, like all arts, we can only improve through practice. We become skillful at taking action by taking action. What do you need to do next?

The Art of Taking Action

Introduction

"Action is the antidote to despair."
– JOAN BAEZ

I would like to tell you about a startling new discovery in the mental health field. This new discovery can reduce the incidence and severity of depression. Experience has further shown that it reduced anxiety in nearly every person who tried it. It increases self-esteem, and builds trust in interpersonal relationships.

It dramatically reduces wasted time. This discovery helps people achieve their goals, and is often associated with productivity, a sense of personal satisfaction, and community responsibility. Further study suggests that, when applied within family settings, households tend to be more organized, and families who live in them less dysfunctional. An examination of speech patterns indicates that people who tried this new discovery spent less time talking about their problems, and more time taking constructive action to solve them.

There are only a few side effects. Many of those who have used this new discovery experience periods of fatigue, which generally go away after a good night's sleep. Other side effects include waves of happiness, joy or satisfaction as a project is finished or a problem solved. These waves of happiness also tend to pass, over time, as one's attention moves to a new purpose. Perhaps the most serious side effect is the potential for arrogance or feelings of superiority and pride that can come with extended use. (There is an antidote for this, which is discussed elsewhere in this book.)

If this new discovery were a pill, it would be put on a fast track to get approval from the FDA, and it would dominate the new genre of pharmaceutical commercials that encourage you to "ask your doctor about it."

But it's not a pill. It's not even a new form of therapy. In fact, using it requires no assistance from a medical or mental health professional. The new discovery is --

Taking Action:

Doing what needs to be done
When it needs to be done
In response to the needs of the situation.

Are you disappointed? Perhaps you were expecting the discovery to be a bit more mysterious, or rooted in scientific advances about the brain, or emanating from the depths of the cosmic psyche. But don't discount the power of taking action. The traditional mental health system has generally overlooked this approach in lieu of talk therapy, self-analysis, dream interpretation, and so forth. Yet the ability to get things done has tremendous healing power. If we look at some of our acknowledged "heroes" of the past — people like Mother Teresa, Martin Luther King, Benjamin Franklin, Eleanor Roosevelt, Albert Schweitzer, Albert Einstein — we find they all were good at taking action. In fact, they are remembered, and honored, for what they did.

But is getting things done really a key element of good mental health? Well, just look at some of the problems associated with not getting things done:

ANXIETY (How am I ever going to get this project done on time?)

DEPRESSION (I haven't really accomplished anything meaningful this whole year.)

INTERPERSONAL CONFLICT (You're not carrying your fair share of the work around here.)

LOSS OF TRUST (You promised you would take care of it, and you didn't. I can't trust you to do what you say.)

SLEEP PROBLEMS (Instead of sleeping, I'm lying here thinking of all the things I have to do.)

LOW SELF-ESTEEM (I can't seem to finish what I start. I'm such a failure.)

ANGER (I'm angry at myself for not getting started on this earlier and waiting until the last minute.)

Taking action is one of the most important skills you can master if you wish to maintain good mental health. And over the course of your lifetime you'll accomplish much more than if you often procrastinate or leave things unfinished. Furthermore, you'll discover new purposes as they are revealed in tasks that are placed in front of you. And by responding to the needs of life around you, whether it be a hungry bird or a thirsty tomato plant, you'll find your place in the interdependent web of life -- a web in which you are not the center

How Do You Know What Action to Take?

Most of our problems fall into one of two categories.

Either we know what needs to be done, and we're not doing it.

or...

We really just don't know what to do.

The first category is by far the most common. You may need to get more exercise, stop smoking, clean your apartment, or go to bed earlier.

Nothing mysterious here. You know what you need to do and you're not doing it.

Talking about what you need to do, researching your options, making a plan, going to therapy, ruminating about your inaction -- these can all be effective strategies for *avoiding* what you know needs doing. The bottom line is you know what to do and you just need to do it!

The second category is a bit trickier. Should you stay in your current job or take that new job offer in Boston? Should you stay in this new relationship or stop now before you get too involved? Should you opt for traditional treatment for your cancer or choose the path of alternative medicine? These types of problems aren't as common as the first group, but they can be confusing and leave you stuck in the world of indecision.

Even if you have plenty of items on your to-do list, you still need to ask the question, "How do I know what needs to be done?" Why? Because being busy doesn't necessarily mean you're doing what's important, or what's needed, or what's meaningful. In fact, one of the most common situations we find ourselves in is getting a lot of urgent things done, while the more important or meaningful items are pushed onto the back burner or simply avoided altogether because we're... well ... "too busy."

If your main problem is that you know what to do but you're not doing it, then your solution is simple – Take Action! Of course, you may have struggled with this challenge for years, which is why you're reading this book. This book will give you everything you need to know to take action. What it won't do is take the action for you. The ultimate solution to your inaction is ... taking action. It's a skill and a habit, and the more you do it, the better you will get at it.

But before you take action, you need to know what action to take.

What Is Your Purpose?

Asking yourself "What is my purpose?" is a good way to check on whether what you are doing is what really needs to be done. But beware. This is a dangerous question. If you ask it while watching TV, surfing the Web, or reading a romance novel, you may be hard-pressed to come up with a justification for what you're doing. You may find that there's little worth to an activity, and many other things to do that are much more purposeful and much more important. These other activities may require more effort, they may be less fun, and they may be more difficult or complex. But they may be more in line with some useful purpose. So perhaps it's time to stop doing what you're doing and start doing something else.

More than 20 years ago, when I became self-employed, I set up a home office. On most days I would go out for lunch, often just for the change of scenery. Sometimes I would use the trip to do some necessary errands, like stopping at a pharmacy or dropping off mail at the post office. If you can tackle these tasks during the same outing you can be a bit more efficient and save yourself some time. But inevitably I would walk past a bookstore, and wander in to browse some new books. Or maybe I would see a sale sign at the local garden center and stop in to get some flowers for the yard. And it couldn't hurt to spend a few extra minutes at the local coffee shop and glance at the newspaper. Or stop by the bike shop. Or the bakery. The lunch hour could easily become the lunch "afternoon."

I "cured" myself of these impulsive explorations by continuing to remind myself of my purpose. If my purpose was to get lunch and drop off the mail, then anything else was a distraction. Bookstores, bakeries and bike shops could wait for evenings and days off. As I stuck more closely to my purpose, it became clearer what needed to be done and what didn't need to be done.

"But what about spontaneity? What about just abandoning ourselves to the moment and enjoying life?" Well, I'm a big fan of spontaneity. I'm also a big fan of joy and flexibility. But most of us are much better at spontaneity than we are at self-discipline. We find it relatively easy to be distracted. We find it much more difficult to stay involved and focused on what we know we need to do.

So don't give up spontaneity. And certainly don't abandon joy and flexibility. Just get better at self-discipline. If you're not taking the action you need to take, then self-discipline is a skill you need to cultivate.

Reflect on Your Life

Were you ever involved in an incident in which you thought you did nothing wrong or inappropriate, but upon further reflection realized that you had caused some discomfort or inconvenience to the other person? Gradually you felt some remorse or guilt over your own conduct, and decided to apologize. Perhaps you wrote a letter of apology, or picked up the phone and called the other person. This is a simple example of how self-reflection can help you know what needs to be done.

But many of us have such busy lives that we don't take time to reflect on what we're doing. We go from one task to the next without pausing to consider what is truly important. Momentum is a double-edged sword. It can help us move forward on an exercise program or a project. But it can also blind us to meaningful questions about our choices, our conduct, and the use of our time. What is the impact of what I'm doing on the world around me? Is this the most important thing for me to be doing? Are my choices consistent with my greater purposes or values? Is there a better way to do this – a kinder way to do this?

These types of questions require self-reflection. Self-reflection allows us to pause, step back, and consider what we have done and where we're headed.

Sometimes a vacation or a formal retreat can give you a new perspective on your life and your work. You may decide that it is time for a change of jobs, or even careers. You may decide to relocate. Or to learn to play the piano. Distance can help you see your life more clearly and decide what needs doing. Distance provides perspective. It's like creating a garden, putting plant after plant in the ground. Digging, planting, digging, planting. But at some point it's helpful to walk to the end of the garden and look around. See the bigger picture. You may learn about placement, about sunlight, or about drainage — things that you wouldn't see crouching down and putting in the next plant.

The most effective method we've found for self-reflection is called Naikan and originated in Japan. It is a simple method that involves three questions:

1. What have I received from__?

2. What have I given to__?

3. What troubles and difficulties have I caused_?

Naikan self-reflection often inspires a greater appreciation for what you have received from others and a natural desire to repay those people for what they have given you. This natural desire to repay others will often give you new or different ideas about what you need to do. Also, Naikan self-

breakers. They were risk-takers in the best sense of the word; they dared to be different."

So as you move into the next year of your life, will you be willing to take a risk in order to discover and live out your purpose? There's really not a safe way to do this. If you want to learn to dive, at some point you need to jump into the water. It's a long way down. You won't do it perfectly the first time, or even the second. Make friends with fear and anxiety, for they're likely to join you on your adventure. And nagging self-doubt is normal. Most people have doubts when they venture into something new. Be wary of plans which involve long waits — retirement or when the kids are all in college. We don't even know what our situation will be tomorrow, let alone 5 years from now.

The biggest risk you can take is to do nothing at all, when you know there's something you need to do. It doesn't seem like a big risk right now, but when you've reached the end of your life, and look back with regret on what you didn't do, then it's too late. You're out of time.

Perhaps this next year of life should come with a warning label:

> **WARNING:**
>
> **Inaction and security may be**
>
> **hazardous to your purpose!**

"Ironically, those who play it safe may be in the greatest danger. When we don't take risks we get stuck in a rut of safety. Over time, we become trapped inside our own life, like a pearl confined to its shell. Life becomes stale and boring. We grow resentful at ourselves for letting our grand passions languish. We tell ourselves, there's got to be something more out there for me. But we know we'll never find it unless we take more risks."

- Bill Treasurer

The Psychology of Action from Japan

Morita Therapy

A Japanese psychiatrist named Shoma Morita, M.D. (1874-1938) developed a model of psychology now known as Morita Therapy in the early part of the 20th century. Rooted in Zen and borrowing from an Eastern world view, it is an approach that fosters action. Let's look at four key elements of Morita Therapy.

I.   *Acceptance at the Heart of Action*

A monk asked Master Dongshan,
"Cold and heat descend upon us. How can we avoid them?"
Dongshan answered, "Why don't you go to the place where there is no cold or heat?"
The monk continued, "Where is the place where there is no cold or heat?"

Dongshan said, "When it is cold, let it be so cold that it kills you. When it is hot, let it be so hot that it kills you."

Generally, when we are in conditions that we find unpleasant we try to manipulate the conditions so they align with our own preferences and desires. If it is hot, we put air conditioning in our homes and cars. If it is humid, we use a dehumidifier. If it is cold, we turn up the furnace so we're nice and toasty and don't venture out unless we have to. We do our best to manipulate the environment to provide the greatest comfort possible.

When we find ourselves in situations that stimulate emotional discomfort, we immediately look to escape from the discomfort just as if it was summer heat or winter cold. We often use one of three strategies: Avoidance, Resignation or Complaining.

Avoidance

This involves trying to escape from our feelings/thoughts – avoiding what is uncomfortable and pursuing what is comfortable. We may try to "cheer up" or take a bath to help us feel relaxed or watch TV or recite affirmations. Regardless of the method, our goal is to replace discomfort with comfort. This is a goal shared by many forms of Western psychotherapy. We want to feel confident, relaxed, and happy. The avoidance strategy doesn't involve acceptance at all, but rather resistance. We resist our emotional experience and devote great energy and attention to trying to manipulate ourselves into a different state. Unfortunately, the resistance itself nurtures a kind of discomfort. And the preoccupation with our internal experience (thoughts and feelings) tends to intensify our suffering while distracting us from activity that can give our life meaning and purpose.

Resignation

We may accept our emotional state and take no action whatsoever. This is a type of acceptance that is really resignation. It is what happens when the depressed person realizes he or she is depressed and then continues to lie on the sofa all afternoon in a state of melancholy. There is a Japanese term, "akirame," that characterizes this approach, and differentiates it from Morita's idea of acceptance. In resignation, we are not trying to escape from our feelings, we are simply languishing in them. Rather than stepping back and observing our feelings we are overcome by them. Our internal experience dictates our conduct and our lives turn into roller coasters as they become mirror images of the constant fluctuations of our feelings.

Complaining

On a hot summer day I asked my seven year old daughter . . .

"Who is hotter – a person who constantly complains throughout the day about how hot it is or a person who doesn't complain?"

She answered, without hesitation, that the person who complained would be hotter. Most of us, even children, how that complaining doesn't help but we continue anyway. When we grudgingly accept our circumstances, we may nevertheless continue to resist our experience by consistently complaining about it. We may accept that it is hot, and we may continue to go about our work, but our experience is punctuated by complaint after complaint which reminds others how uncomfortable we are and reminds ourselves how much we wish things were different than they are.

"Paradoxically, this practice of complaining increases clients' suffering. The more they detail their complaints, the more they focus their attention upon the complaints."
- Shoma Morita, M.D.

Arugamama

Arugamama is the term Morita used to describe the state of acceptance. It means "to accept things as they are." Perhaps it comes closest to Dongshan's advice in the above Zen koan. When we are hot, we just let ourselves be hot. When we are anxious, we just let ourselves feel anxiety. When we are depressed, we just allow ourselves to feel depressed and hopeless. *The state of arugamama is one in which we do not try to escape from our emotional experience*. We are not seeking any kind of emotional or cognitive state other than the one we are in at the moment. Yet we continue to devote ourselves to what is important for us to do. We carry out the purposes of our lives, because they give life meaning. In *arugamama* we find the quality of non-resistance, similar to what is taught in many forms of martial arts. When our opponent is bigger or stronger, direct resistance is ineffective. So we learn to use our opponent's energy against him. Through non-resistance, a small person can defeat a larger and stronger person. Through non-resistance, a weak-willed person can defeat anxiety or depression. It is not necessary to conquer or overpower our depression. We accept the experience of depression and make no effort to escape. And we invite depression to accompany us while we make dinner, or go shopping or walk the dog. Our anxiety is our companion as we make our presentation to a room full of people.

Most of the tasks and challenges we face stimulate mental and emotional processes. Fear, anxiety, boredom, frustration or lack of confidence may accompany us at any time. Of course we often idealize what our internal experience should be.

"I shouldn't be so worried about my exam."

"I shouldn't be so upset about the feedback I received."

When we are caught up in our idealized views about how we should be, we cannot accept things as they are. It is like the monk saying, "It shouldn't be so hot. It's already September." But at this moment it is this hot. It's just as hot as it is. So to practice this state of *arugamama* we have to allow the heat to "kill" us. This doesn't mean that we literally die. It means that we are "consumed" by the heat to such a degree that we are completely hot. There is no resistance, no complaint, no effort to escape. The Buddhist teacher Pema Chodron has written a book called "The Wisdom of No Escape." What a wonderful title (and a wonderful book, too).

At one point in my life I was facing a great dilemma. Through a series of foolish choices I had created a situation that would create great suffering for someone, as well as for myself, no matter what choice I made. For months I refused to accept the reality of this situation and struggled for a way out, an escape that would be free of discomfort and anxiety. But I couldn't find such a solution. My clever mind, which had served me so well in the past, could not find a way out. No matter which way I turned I would encounter, and cause, great suffering. So I remained paralyzed, trapped by inaction and constant rumination. Then one day it hit me: *Suffering was inevitable. There was no escape.* I accepted this premise, not just intellectually, but with my whole being. There was no escape! And when I realized this, I took action. I took the next step. And, of course, pain and suffering followed. But I was able to accept the situation as it was. And I've had to live with the karma that I created. But life had to continue, to move forward. *Arugamama* allows us to move forward, because we are "consumed" by the heat, consumed by "things as they are." When we stop trying to escape from things as they are, we can move forward and live in a more natural and meaningful way.

Generally, we think of acceptance being in opposition to action. But Morita's view of acceptance is that it is very connected to action. In fact, we might say that acceptance – of our internal human condition as well as external conditions – is at the very heart of action.

II.   *The Uncontrollable Nature of our Thoughts and Feelings*

One of the main tenets of Morita Therapy is that our internal experience (feelings and thoughts) is basically uncontrollable by our will. If we feel anxious about going for a job interview we can't necessarily make ourselves feel relaxed and confident. If filling out income tax forms feels frustrating and tedious, we can't just snap our fingers and suddenly find the task satisfying and exciting. Worried thoughts arise despite our desire to avoid them. Worried feelings manifest themselves as butterflies in our stomach, sweat on our palms or a tightness around our neck. If we're depressed we're told to "cheer up" or "think positively" but we find that both strategies are often ineffective. They're ineffective because our thoughts have a mind of their own. They pretty much come and go as they please. And our feelings also arise naturally and spontaneously. We hear a new song and we enjoy listening to it. We meet someone at a social gathering and feel an attraction.

In fact, a Princeton University study found that we respond so rapidly and intuitively to faces (less than one second) that our rational minds really have no time to influence the reaction.

"Trying to control the emotional self willfully by manipulative attempts is like trying to choose a number on a thrown die or pushing back the water of the Kamo river upstream. Certainly, we end up aggravating our agony and feeling unbearable pain because of our failure in manipulating the emotions."

—Shoma Morita, M.D.

Anybody who has meditated for long periods of time knows how "wild" the mind can be. During meditation we watch how the mind unfolds from moment to moment, so we become familiar with the process. But the process is no different off the meditation cushion than it is on the cushion.

"… a person who is obsessed with the desire for perfect feelings tries to feel refreshed at all times. In fact, however, our daily feelings naturally flow and change according to internal and external conditions like the weather. A person who insists upon feeling refreshed is like one who hopes to have clear skies all the time. As soon as he sees a bit of a cloud he assumes the weather will be terrible all day. When he feels just a little out of sorts he tells himself that he is no good and he makes himself feel worse."

- Takahisa Kora, M.D.

My wife used to run a psychiatric rehabilitation center for people with mental illness. One day we conducted an experiment. We invited people to come outside for a picnic lunch in which we were going to talk honestly about "all the crazy thoughts in our heads." A group of about eight of us gathered around the tables. I started by telling a true story in which I was driving south on a two lane highway in Vermont, about 20 miles from my home.

It was early evening and as I headed south I noted an oncoming vehicle heading north with its headlights on. I had the thought,

"If I just turn the steering wheel two inches I could be dead in a matter of seconds."

I looked at the faces around me. Several of them appeared surprised, even shocked, that I would have such thoughts. "What happened?" asked a 30 year old man who was schizophrenic.

"Well, I just noticed the thought and kept on driving home," I said.

For those with mental illness, this thought was a "symptom" — something to be concerned about, perhaps requiring assistance from a mental health professional. People with mental illness are often surprised to find that the rest of us have "crazy" thoughts that arise periodically. We have sexual thoughts, adulterous thoughts, suicidal thoughts, mean thoughts, vengeful thoughts, grandiose thoughts—and plenty of thoughts which have little, if anything, to do with the reality around us.

Morita's work provides great relief as we begin to see these thoughts as *happening to us*, similar to the way rain falls or a gust of wind blows across the yard. Generally we have been taught that such thoughts are "bad" and that we should avoid them. But the effort to avoid them requires a tremendous amount of energy and often we find that while we can consciously shift our thoughts in a given moment, we have little or no control over what thoughts pop up in the next moment. Even the thought, "I shouldn't have such thoughts about others. I should think more kindly towards others," is an uncontrollable thought when it first arises.

Morita's premise—that our thoughts and feelings are mostly uncontrollable—leads to his prescription:

Accept your thoughts and feelings.

Rather than fight what goes on in your mind, simply accept it.

III. *Action and Intention*

Let's consider *action* and *intention* from a Morita Therapy perspective. What is an INTENTION? Right now I'm sitting on the porch of the ToDo Institute in Vermont and I intend to get up and get something to drink. So really, my intention is simply a thought. I'm having the thought, "I think I'll go into the kitchen and get a cold drink." I may also *feel* a bit thirsty (which I am). But if you were to watch me as this is happening you would neither know that I'm thirsty or be aware that I am thinking of getting a drink. You would simply see me staring at my laptop screen and typing from time to time. My intention is very personal and private. You can't see it and it arguably has no effect on the world around me. The thought, "I'll go and get a drink" might easily be followed by other thoughts about what I'm writing, or the fly on my wrist, or how sweet my dog looks sleeping next to me, none of which we would really consider intentions.

What distinguishes an intentional thought from other thoughts is that it's a thought which has the idea of a future action. Notice I said "the idea" of a future action.

Now suppose I do get up to get a drink (I haven't yet, but I'm still thinking about it). Now I'm engaged in ACTION. My body is moving. There are kinesthetic, chemical and electrical changes happening in my body. My dog has noticed my movement so I'm having some type of impact on the world. I'm creating friction and erosion on the wood beneath my feet as I walk. I may even be killing living creatures (bugs) as I move from one place to another. If you were watching me, you may not know where I'm going, but you'd know I'm walking. My action has become an observable fact that clearly has some impact on my environment.

In Morita therapy it's very important for us to recognize the distinction between thoughts (which include intentional thoughts) and actions. There is a world of difference between the two, just as there is a world of difference between a photograph of a blueberry pie and an actual blueberry pie. Personally, I'd rather have one small forkful of an actual pie, than an 8 x 10 photo of the entire pie. Good intentions are wonderful but I'd rather have a small portion of compassionate action than a barn full of ideas about kindness. Intentions don't necessarily result in action, and 92 percent (or more) of us have learned that from our experience with New Year's resolutions.

I'm not suggesting that intentions don't have value. In some cases they are clearly precursors to actions, perhaps even noble or selfless actions. But in many cases they are not. Intentions may influence how we act, though of greater importance may be how our actions influence our intentions. Inevitably we must abandon the idea that INTENTIONS, even particularly strong, clear or meaningful intentions, will lead us to action.

IV.   What Does Lead to Action?

This is the million dollar question! If we could just act every time we had an intentional thought we'd be doing great! Well, probably not. There are times when we have intentional thoughts and our lack of action works in our favor. Suppose you are married but meet an attractive person at a conference. Lots of intentional thoughts drift through your mind:

I'll call her room and ask her to dinner.

I'll suggest we go out someplace tomorrow night.

I'll tell her how attracted I am to her.

But you don't act on any of these thoughts and that saves your marriage. It's not that we want a magic pill that will help us act on our thoughts. Rather, we want to be able to act, or not act, according to our purposes. If one of our purposes is to stay healthy, we want to be able to make healthful choices and develop habits that support a healthy body and mind.

Some literature suggests that you reward yourself when you take the action you know you should take. "If I meditate every morning for a week I'll reward myself by getting a massage." Sometimes this may work, but it doesn't help us develop self-discipline or a purpose-centered approach to life. Nor will establishing negative rewards (punishments) when we fail.

What we really want to do is develop

a natural approach to taking action that meets

the needs of the situation.

Morita Therapy is a wonderful approach that help us cut through many of the excuses, explanations and stories about why we aren't doing what we need to be doing in our lives. It's an empowering method that gives us choices for how to respond to challenges other than simply reacting to our feeling state.

Kaizen

"A journey of a thousand miles begins with the first step." — *Lao Tzu*

In June of 2006, Harriet, a giant tortoise, died at the ripe old age of 176. She was reportedly one of several giant tortoises that Charles Darwin collected on his visit to the Galapagos Islands. Harriet was a domed tortoise. She lived on an island that was fairly wet, where a domed tortoise had an easy time finding and munching on local grasses. Harriet had cousins called saddleback tortoises. The shells of these tortoises evolved in such a way that the tortoises could stretch their necks upwards and graze on above-ground cactus plants. This was necessary because the climate on the islands where they live is much drier, so ground grasses are not readily available.

This adaptation didn't happen instantly. It happened over millions of years. That's a timeframe that probably isn't well suited to most of us when it comes to making changes in our lives. We want to lose 20 pounds, not over the next year, but over the next month. We want to meet someone and fall in love with him or her and have a wonderful, romantic relationship, not sometime in the next 25 years, but during the next few weeks. We want to become proficient at a martial art, or foreign language, or watercolor painting. But that proficiency must happen quickly, for our minds have very little patience for gradual learning and gradual change. Yet the general principle of what Darwin called "gradualism" — incremental changes over time — may give hope to those of us who have consistently tried and failed to make colossal changes in our habits or lifestyle.

About 92% of those who make New Year's resolutions fail to keep them. So if you have had clear, healthy intentions to do something, and haven't made good on your commitment, you have lots of company. Unfortunately, our impatient minds are at odds with the natural laws of the universe. Change is the rule, not the exception — but most change comes gradually, over time. Rarely do we make a big jump from Point A to Point B in a week or a month. Much of the change that takes place in our behavior is so gradual that we hardly notice it, just as a mother may not be aware of how much her child has grown in the past year.

Continuous Improvement

In Japan there is an approach towards company improvement called "kaizen." It's a generic Japanese word that means "improvement," but is usually used to describe a program of organizational development that is based on "continuous improvement." The program originated in Depression-era America and was later imported into Japan as the U.S. made an effort to support Japan's reconstruction after WWII. One of the main proponents of Kaizen was Dr. W. Edwards Deming, who was invited to consult with Japan on their country's productivity and efficiency. In a business setting, some of the key features of Kaizen are continuous improvement, worker participation, and a humanized approach to increased productivity.

In his book *One Small Step Can Change Your Life*, psychologist Robert Maurer discusses the Kaizen principles as they may be applied to personal change. The basic strategy is that you start out by making a very small change, and then build and build on that small change until, eventually, you end up with significant progress.

"Small actions take very little time or money, and they are agreeable even to those of us who haven't laid up bulk supplies of willpower. Small actions trick the brain into thinking: Hey, this change is so tiny that it's no big deal. No need to get worked up. No risk of failure or unhappiness here. By outfoxing the fear response, small actions allow the brain to build up new, permanent habits—at a pace that may be surprisingly brisk."

- Robert Maurer

The Kaizen strategy goes one step beyond "showing up," because you actually have to do something. But what you have to do is minimal. Suppose you're trying to get your garden in shape. Your first step might be to go out to the garden and pull one weed and plant one tomato plant. That seems insignificant . . . and that's the point. Start with actions that are so small, so insignificant, that there's no resistance, no reason to procrastinate or avoid the task. But Kaizen is about continuous improvement, so the next day you might pick 3 weeds and plant 2 plants. Over a period of weeks you end up making great progress in your garden. Maurer offers an example of how Kaizen works:

"I've seen people who simply will not, cannot, floss their teeth. They know they're at risk for tooth decay and gum disease, and they feel they ought to develop a flossing habit, but they can't seem to translate that knowledge into action. So I've asked them to floss one tooth a day. These people find this tiny step much easier. After a month of flossing one tooth every day, they have two things: one very clean tooth and a habit of picking up that silly string."

Kaizen is about making changes over time. It's the personal version of Darwin's theory of evolution. It's the way we accumulate savings in a bank account with compound interest. There is excitement in winning the lottery or making a "killing" in the stock market. Many of us want that kind of victory when it comes to losing weight, writing a book or learning to play music.

But if you look at the natural world you will see that change is more likely to come incrementally. Our perennial plants expand their territory a few inches every spring. And each year there's a segment of new growth on the evergreen tree's branches. And then there's the tortoise — known, in fable, as the slowpoke in the race. Small, painstakingly slow steps—one after another. Without speed, without spurts, without sprints, they seem to get where they want to go. Small steps—but constant and consistent. And perhaps the tortoise's pace and patience have something to do with their lifespan — a respectable 176 years for old Harriet.

Life refuses to stay the same. People get gray hair or lose it altogether. Puppies get big. Wood rots. Pianos go out of tune and metal rusts. Change is the rule. But fast, immediate, dramatic change is usually not the rule. Volcanoes and earthquakes remind us that nature can make exceptions to any rule. But for us, conscious change may well require some simple, basic ingredients – have a clear purpose, show up, take small steps, repeat this formula daily, and be patient.

Naikan

The final member of our psychological trio is an approach called Naikan, which means "inside looking." It is a method of self-reflection that has its roots in Shin Buddhism from Japan. Naikan was developed by Yoshimoto Ishin, a businessman and devout Buddhist who wanted to offer a process of self-reflection that would be accessible to people in daily life. Naikan provides a systematic approach to reflecting on ourselves and our relationships that helps us appreciate the ways we are being cared for and supported, many of which we take for granted during the course of an ordinary day. It also helps us become aware of the impact our lives are having on the world around us. In essence, we get to see ourselves from the world's perspective, instead of our own.

The process of Naikan reflection is relatively simple. It is based on three questions:

(1) What have I received from ____?
(2) What have I given to ____?
(3) What troubles and difficulties have I caused ____?

These questions provide a framework for reflecting on parents, friends, teachers, siblings, colleagues, children and partners. We reflect by answering these questions within a defined period of time. The time period we examine can be as short as a day or as long as three to four years.

We generally consider self-reflection or introspection as the opposite of action. And when I first discovered Naikan, I never really considered its relationship to the theme of action in my life. But I now believe it is very relevant in its influence on the actions we choose to take and how we take those actions in relation to others.

Let's consider the story of a young man who is about to graduate from high school. However, in his last semester at school he makes a foolish choice that can potentially get him into so much trouble that he won't graduate, which means he won't go on to college. A teacher who has been a mentor to him for the past few years steps in and intervenes. His intervention makes it possible for the young man to make amends for the problem he caused and avoid the serious repercussions that would otherwise have awaited him. The young man is both relieved and grateful and, upon graduation, he writes himself a letter. In the letter, he describes the kindness of this teacher and how his intervention made it possible for him to graduate. The young man then goes on to college, and graduates four years later.

After graduation, he returns home. One summer morning he is having a cup of coffee and making a list of things he needs to do that day. There are errands to run, a few items to buy, several calls to old friends, etc. His mother had asked him to clean out a box of papers from high school that have been in the upstairs closet. He decides to spend a few minutes sorting through the papers, and comes across the letter he wrote about the help of his former teacher. It stimulates very strong emotions, and he realizes that he hasn't had contact with his teacher for years. So he decides that one of the things he needs to do is try to get in touch with his teacher and see if he could arrange to take him to lunch.

There's nothing dramatic about this story. It's simply about someone who is reminded of a kindness that was done for him and, as a result, wants to do something in return. However, had he not been reminded by his old letter, his interest in contacting his old teacher might never have arisen.

Naikan is a unique reminder system. By reflecting on our past (perhaps just the past week) we're reminded of something we should do for someone who was supportive or helpful to us. So Naikan is related to action, because it can influence what action we choose to take and when we take it. I have known people who completed a Naikan retreat (one week of about 100 hours of self-reflection) and, as a result, wrote thank-you letters to their dads, set up a time to visit their aging moms, or repaid a sum of money that was years overdue.

Not only does Naikan influence what we do, but it also influences our attitude toward doing it. Sometimes, we face challenges in our lives that require a great deal of time and effort and are confusing and emotionally draining. In such situations, we can feel very alone and even resent having to deal with the challenge. My colleague Julie found herself as the primary caretaker for her 88-year-old mother. She would sleep at her mom's home several nights per week, cook for her, clean the house and even change her mother's diapers. She had a regular practice of Naikan reflection for many years. She told me that from time to time, she would resent having to spend so much time taking care of her mom. But she added that during her Naikan retreat, when reflecting on her years as a child, she had calculated how many of her diapers her mom had changed for her. She said that when she added up the diapers that she had changed for her mom, it wasn't even close to 10 percent. Then she would appreciate having the opportunity to repay her mom, in just a small way, for the care that she had received as a child. Instead of an attitude of resentment, Naikan helped her bring an attitude of love and service to her mother's care.

Naikan helps reveal the support we're receiving, even when we think we're doing something alone. Our reflection reveals the presence of inanimate objects or tools that help us do our work. When we're cleaning a room, we are grateful to have rags, towels, brooms, a dustpan, cleanser, and a vacuum. We're never really doing work on our own; we're always part of a larger team, seen and unseen, that makes it possible to do what we do.

As we age, we discover that our physical capacity for action gradually diminishes. Over time we become less capable of moving fast, of lifting heavy objects . . . even the ability to see what we're doing can decline. This isn't a pleasant idea, but for most of us it will be true. At the age of 25, we may resent having to clean out the garage. But at the age of 85, we would be grateful to have the strength and stamina to do it just one more time.

Self-reflection can help us appreciate the capacity to do our work, and to bring that sense of appreciation to the work itself. To mow the lawn and be grateful for the mower, for the lawn and even for the ability we possess to walk back and forth while pushing the mower – that is what self-reflection offers us. It's a way of action that goes beyond just checking something off our to-do list.

Morita therapy, Kaizen, Naikan – each of these methods offers us some wisdom about what action to take and how to take it. They are like three wise, old teachers offering guidance as we try to do something meaningful within the limits of a lifetime.

Inaction

Deciding Is Not Doing

Have you ever been in a quandary and, after considering different options and possibilities, you finally decided what you needed to do?

This often happens to me. I try to decide where to go for a week's vacation in August. I try to decide what kind of siding to put on the teahouse the ToDo Institute is building up the hill. I consider what type of software platform would be best for our new website. Let's say I am looking back at the day and making a list of what I did:

1. Decided to send the girls to the Adventure camp instead of soccer camp.
2. Decided to fix my old mountain bike instead of buying a new one.
3. Decided not to get the girls a trampoline.(They're not going to like this.)
4. Decided on the type of border to use in the garden alongside the driveway.
5. Decided to try to set up a dinner near Woodstock,

Vermont with our old friend Kathy while she is temporarily working there.

6. Decided to go up to Home Depot on Saturday and get the materials I need to finish the new wall, which I put up last year.

Wow! I really made a lot of progress today, didn't I?

Well, it <u>feels</u> like I did. There are some decisions that are extremely important and require a fair amount of consideration. Trying to decide on the proper software platform and design for a website is clearly important. I remember when we were trying to decide whether or not to adopt a child. *That* decision had a dramatic effect on my entire life.

But we shouldn't confuse deciding **with acting.** If you were to watch me making decisions, mostly you would see me

JUST SITTING THERE.

I might be looking something up on the Web or surveying the grounds, but what you would see me doing is really... not very much.

And -- this is critical -- the difference in reality before and after the decision is...

NO DIFFERENCE.

Until I actually take some constructive action, I have not changed the reality of my life or the world around me at all by just deciding. It may seem like progress. It certainly feels like progress. But keep in mind that regardless of how much thought and energy went into that decision, I can change it in an instant. I can simply think,

"No, I think I'll do something else instead."

Now I've made two decisions, and still nothing has changed.

So please be cautious about thinking of decision-making as something you did. Generally, it's something you thought. *Writing the first paragraph of your book… or planting some basil in the garden … or filing papers with the adoption office in China … or riding your bicycle for ten minutes.* These are actions.

These are the things that create

ripples in our lives –

and in the world.

And those ripples can end up traveling great distances in both time and space as they change lives in ways that cannot be predicted.

"Consider the implications of a life in which you don't have the power, focus, or single-mindedness to do what you say you will do. Imagine the countless times your wiser self decides on a particular course of action, only to be blown off course by the merest breeze of immediate desire. There's a helplessness, a scattered, drifting quality about such a life."

— DAN ROSENTHAL

To Merely Want to Do Something Is Not Enough

SHINICHI SUZUKI

Life was wretched in Japan right after the end of World War II. The winters in Matsumoto are severe, and there are days when the temperature falls to 13 or 18 degrees below zero centigrade. On one of those days my sister returned from an errand, and, as she shook off the snow, she said, "In all this cold, there is a wounded soldier standing on the bridge down by Honmachi, begging. He is standing there shivering in this driving snow, and nobody is putting any money in the box at his feet… I wanted to invite him in to sit in our kotatsu in our warm room and give him some tea."

I immediately replied, "You merely wanted to?"

She answered yes, and suddenly ran out into the street. I made the room warmer, stirred up the fire in the kotatsu, got out some cookies somebody had sent us as a gift, and waited. About thirty minutes later my sister came back with the white-clad, wounded soldier. "This lady insisted…" he began to explain.

"You are very welcome; do come in." Koji and I urged him into the kotatsu with us, and we sat and talked about all sorts of things. Finally he asked me for the second time, "Why are you so kind to me?"

"My sister happened to see you," I replied, "and insisted on inviting you in."

"It's the first time anyone has… and today was so cold and miserable," he said.

He told us about his experience in the war, and how he was going from place to place collecting money for the wounded soldiers, and we talked and talked for three hours, until he got warm again. He then got up, saying he had to go to Nagano. At the front door, in spite of his protestations that I already had been far too kind, I put some money in his box, saying jokingly that it was just compensation for causing him to lose a half day's business, and anyway it was not his own personal box and so he had no right to refuse.

Afterward, my sister said to me, "You taught me an excellent lesson." Indeed, it was our first exercise in "If you want to do something, do it."

Plenty of people often think, "I'd like to do this, or that." We all have the ability to think that. But it usually ends there, and people who put their thoughts into practice are very few indeed. I realized I was one of those people who just think of doing things, and made a resolution:

"There is no merit in just thinking about doing something. The result is exactly the same as not thinking about it. It is only doing the thing that counts. I shall acquire the habit of doing what I have in mind to do."

Why is it that so many people think of doing things and do not do them? Why do they not have the power to put into practice the things they think of doing? If one just thinks about it, the chance slips by. From the time they are children, people are ordered about by their parents to do this, to do that. They develop resistance, and reluctantly do as they are told, or avoid doing it if possible. The resistance habit becomes subconscious, until they are unable to perform immediately even those things they think of doing themselves. They may think something is a good thing to do, but they have gotten so that they are unable to do it simply and naturally. People lose a great deal this way.

"We should have done it. It was such a good chance, but we let it slip by." Because they are incapable of putting thoughts into action straight away time after time, people's destiny never develops. They close the stable door after the horse is gone. Chances come to everyone. Yes, chances come; but we don't grasp them. By not claiming them we renounce them.

"I should write a letter" — "I should reply to a letter." If you think so, write immediately. You are not doing anything at the time but just think you will wait and do it later. Even small tasks should not be neglected, but completed right away. It is very important to be able to do this. *People who get a lot done manage it because they have the ability to get each necessary thing done right there and then.* If you put a task off until some other time, you will never get it done, because "some other time" has its own tasks. Consequently you end up doing nothing and become a person who keeps putting things off. Time doesn't wait; but most people are *so narigachi na no desu* (not up to doing things).

The habit of action — this, I think, is the most important thing we must acquire. Life's success or failure actually depends on this one thing. So what should we do? We should get so that it is second nature to put our thoughts into action. Start now, today. True, it is easier to say than to do, but the more you do it, the more of a habit it will become. It is an indispensable skill. To know something and not to put it into practice is a weak point, but knowledge is mere knowledge, and is not to be confused with ability and skill. Not until knowledge becomes an inseparable part of one is it an ability or skill. There are plenty of people who know a lot about baseball and can criticize a game; however, the spectator lacks the intuitive skills, judgment, and physical coordination of the experienced player.

A fine society is not built by people who just think about what is right to do. What we need are people with the ability of the experienced baseball player, people with various deeply inculcated skills.

Shinichi Suzuki (1898-1998) was the founder of the Suzuki Talent Education method—a method used throughout the world to teach children to love and play music and to cultivate the heart-mind (kokoro) of the individual.

The Stress of Not Getting Things Done

TRUDY BOYLE

Stress is getting a lot of hype lately, and after reading several articles on the subject, I've concluded that one sure way to increase my stress is to read about it. With diabetes, heart disease, ulcers, hypertension, sexual difficulties, and a compromised immune system the consequences of living in an increasingly stressful world is scary. Most of us have busy lives, and demands on our time, money, and creativity leave little room for maneuvering. What hope is there for us to reduce our stress? Are we really so ill-equipped to deal with daily life?

Dr. Hans Selye, a leading authority on stress, provides reassurance that we are not only well equipped to cope with daily stressors but more importantly we can use our behavior to reduce the type of distress that is harmful. "Stress is the spice of life," he says, "and arises from pleasant as well as unpleasant activities." Our goal need not be freedom from all stress -- that would mean death – but rather to live in such a way as to minimize the stress that is most harmful.

What kind of approach does Selye recommend? Rather than the typical stress reduction activities, which are so highly publicized, his guidelines are more like a fundamental code of everyday living:

- know your long-range purposes

- work in the service of some cause that you can respect

- attempt to live and work in an environment in line with your own innate values

- develop a philosophy of gratitude

- reduce procrastination – it can be dangerous

- use muscular activity to alleviate frustration

- understand that aimlessness causes harmful stress

- work itself is good and a basic life necessity

The Stress Triangle

My number one stress creator is not completing a task I have set for myself or following through promptly. The stress is compounded when I take on more than I can deliver in the allotted time. And my final penchant, which makes up what I call my "stress triangle," is to ignore the whole lot until the last sixty seconds!

How do I let this controllable stress occur? The honest answer is that I sometimes let my feelings boss me around. One of the puzzling lessons I have learned is that, more often than not, I do not feel like doing most of the things that need doing. I'm not just speaking about cleaning the toilet bowl or doing my tax return. I'm referring to those things that I genuinely desire to accomplish like writing, preparing courses, learning calligraphy. I haven't yet felt in the mood to get out of my cozy bed early in the morning on a dark rainy day, and get started on my goals. The "writing feeling" does not strike me until I'm actually writing.

Pondering why I don't feel like doing what I say I want to do, yet discovering one more time how great it often feels after I've done it, is just another reliable way to distract myself from the effort of doing the next thing. There is no substitute for "accepting my feelings" (of laziness or boredom, or anxiety, or whatever happens to appear), knowing my purpose" and then "DOING IT." My stress is relieved almost from the moment I start, and I go to bed that night satisfied with what got accomplished.

A Penny for Your Stress

Another highly ranked source of stress is money problems. While it can be stressful to have an excess or a deficit of funds, it is the deficits I find most challenging. Adjusting to an ever-declining income can be an exercise in frustration and adaptation. Still, it's less stressful to know where I stand than to trick myself into pretending that things are different than they are. And I can reduce stress even more by spending less than I earn. As Mr. Micawber, a Charles Dickens character, advised David Copperfield, "Annual income twenty pounds, annual expenditure nineteen, nineteen six, result happiness. Annual income twenty pounds, annual expenditure twenty pounds one and six, result misery."

Financial competence and stress reduction walk hand in hand. I keep going back to the basics: acknowledge my feelings (all those endless desires), know my purpose (to live within a budget) and do what I have to do. Knowing my purpose and sticking to it is not a matter of settling for less, but a matter of becoming reliable. I pay careful attention to everyday expenditures. Take meal preparation as an example. I no longer ask myself, "What do I feel like eating tonight?" but rather, "What is a tasty, healthy meal I can prepare in an economical manner?" or "What needs to be eaten in the fridge today?" Learning to cook a delicious dinner without using gourmet ingredients takes skill and creativity and offers more than just food for the body.

Attitude and Action

My mother never spoke to me about stress, only about the normalcy of life's difficulties. She treated obstacles as opportunities. Her response to my complaints, though sympathetic, would be something like, "Learning how to solve problems now is the way to gain confidence for solving bigger problems when you no longer live at home." One of her favorite maxims was, "It's not what happens to you in life that counts, but your attitude and what you do about it." My 68 years of experience validates what she said those many years ago. Her homespun advice kept me off the couch of many a psychiatrist.

Several years ago, when my 23-year-old daughter was in her last year of university, she called me in tears after a major disagreement with her boyfriend. A breakup was imminent, finals were upon her, and she was so stressed out that she couldn't study. "What can I do?" she cried. I listened, asked some questions, expressed my sympathy, and then used some of my mother's philosophy. I asked if her room was messy. It was. I suggested she clean it up before we talk further, and call me when it was done. She called back in 45 minutes and told me how much better she felt, not nearly so stressed out and able to tackle her books.

Cleaning your room isn't a permanent cure for emotional suffering, but the order, and the muscular exercise, are temporarily helpful distractions. When I am filled with emotion, big muscle activity helps reduce my stress. "Physical exertion gives your brain a rest," says Dr. Selye, and "helps us to stop worrying about the frustrating problem."

We often hear the plea for more time out, but Dr. Selye cautions us to resist such temptation. Aimlessness and procrastination create frustration, and the stress of frustration is much more likely than that of excessive muscular work or engrossing mental work, to produce disease." In our current culture of ego-based busyness, however, I suspect that "more time out" is also expressing a need for less distraction. A natural desire to concentrate on one task at a time. And that often depends on us.

For instance, consider the responsible use of the word NO. I am all for YES, in the broadest sense of the word, yet, I understand and have experienced that in a world filled with opportunities for our pleasure, purpose and generosity that we need to choose when to say yes and when to say *"Thank-you for asking. I am honored, but not now. My plate is currently full, and until something comes off there is no room for anything else to go on."* Those words, spoken to me 20 years ago by Barbara Sarah, a friend and colleague, have helped me immeasurably in the slow process of recognizing when my plate is overloaded, and that the appropriate response is not always yes.

Reflective Moments

Still, I find it useful to step back and periodically reflect on my life, and, as my friend Julie Guroff once said, "It's hard to feel stressed out and grateful at the same time." In truth, we are all continually supported.

The specificity of Naikan, when I do it honestly and sincerely, points to a wider image of reality and not just the parts that favor my own self-image. For example, when I am stressed-out over problems, Naikan reflection helps me see the way I waste money and time; assists me to triage my current situation into uncontrollable, controllable, and influenceable chunks. And I also see the support that keeps rolling in, in one form or another. With this realistic self-examination against my own standards, it soon becomes obvious that I have received more from the world than I've given, or could ever return. This knowledge often gives me a different perspective on my current problem and redirects my attention towards some form of action, rather than just worrying.

Conclusion

My life, like most of yours, is not stress-free. However, when I live purposefully and wholeheartedly, my everyday life has more satisfying moments, and I tend not to categorize the rest as stressful or not. It is simply a matter of responding to the needs of the next moment. When I do experience the signs of stress, it is a relief to observe that some of my stressful moments fade with the passage of time; some by exercise; others by reflection, but mostly by looking at what needs doing in my life that I'm not attending to, and getting it done. That offers me true relief.

The Price That Others Pay

LINDA ANDERSON KRECH

It's hard to change. Surprisingly hard, in fact. Even when we are crystal clear about the need to make a change in how we are living, we can easily slip back into an old groove in the blink of an eye. Our default settings have history on their side, and they are fueled by years of momentum. It's not easy.

Take procrastination, for example. Many of us prefer to tolerate the personal consequences and inconvenience that result from procrastination than to face the discomfort and disruption of changing our ways. Fine. It's our karma. It's our life. It's our choice, right? Yes, the choice rests squarely on our shoulders and is ours to make.

The consequences of that choice, however, are another matter. Often we are not the only victim touched by our irresponsible choices and poor time management. Our day-to-day doings and misdoings impact on those we know and those we won't ever know. What sometimes lights a fire beneath us is recognizing the degree to which this is true. This truth can propel us beyond our comfort zone in a way that our own personal suffering never would. Isn't that great? Remembering our impact on others during decisive moments can help us to make a different history for ourselves.

Rushing

Maybe we didn't get started early enough. Maybe we underestimated the time it was going to take. Maybe we were distracted or tired or just not in the mood. Eventually we did what needed to be done, but it wasn't done on time.

If we are late with a task or project, there's a very good chance that in the final moments or days we will start speeding up our engines in an effort to make up for lost time. And during those rushing moments, when we are trying to compress our work into what little time is left, our relationships with others can become strained and delicate.

Minor challenges, such as unanticipated distractions or interruptions, may be uncharacteristically provocative, resulting in friction with others. Frenetic energy can be easily contagious, making it difficult for others around us to relax. Communication problems are also more likely to occur in our haste, as our words and tone of voice may become more impatient. It's hard to be good company when we are in overdrive.

In the aftermath of a rush to the finish line, we may discover, ironically, a new crop of time-consuming problems for us, and others, to deal with. During rush-recovery time we must face the state of affairs that we created in our haste. If we haven't planned enough time to pack and prepare for vacation, for example, we may return home to find a state of chaos that was created due to last minute preparations. The more rushed we are, the more we hone in on the goal and disregard everything else.

And the carelessness that results from all of this rushing can take many forms – we can misplace our keys, spill our coffee, forget our phone or drive too fast. Many mishaps can occur in our attempts to recapture a few extra minutes and reach our goals on time.

Waiting

Here's a quiz. Which is longer -- 15 minutes of waiting for someone who is late, or 15 minutes of keeping others waiting? Objectively, it's the same period of time, but when you have managed to successfully negotiate life on your end and have arrived for your appointment on time (leaving countless other things undone in the process), you can become painfully aware of someone else's inability or unwillingness to do the same.

When we keep others waiting, we are not being respectful of their lives. And time is the most precious commodity that any of us have. Even if they are gracious about waiting for us, even if they use their time well and minimize the trouble they experience, we are still stealing some of their life.

Dominoes

Suppose one day I leave the house late for an early morning dental appointment. I had hoped to call them on the way in, so they could plan accordingly, but I discovered in the car that my phone was dead. I encountered an unexpected traffic jam, due to construction, which set me back even further. It is quite late by the time I arrive at the dentist's.

We are never privy to the ways that our lateness ripples out into the world. We don't get to see the impact, as it bumps up against other people during the course of the day. I may have triggered problems for the dentist by creating tension, or making him keep other patients waiting, which affects his reputation. I may have kept other patients waiting who needed to get back to work, which may have had an effect on their co-workers and their clients. Like dominoes, we can tip into each other with our lateness, setting off a wave of impact that we never get to see, even though we may have set the events into motion.

The Karma of Things Undone

So far, we've looked at the impact of getting things done late. But what about the impact of not getting things done at all?

At least in some cases, someone else will do what I never got around to doing. If it's a household chore, like taking the compost out or folding the laundry, then our spouses or children might pick up the slack. If it's a work project, a colleague might have to add it to an already lengthy task list. In most cases, we will cause less trouble to others by saying "no" in the first place than by taking it on as our responsibility and ultimately leaving it undone. This is tough. It requires good, sound, realistic judgment, which can be hard to come by. Good intentions do not soften the impact of our failure to deliver. In some cases the task simply remains undone, and in its place grows resentment, frustration and disappointment.

Excuses

No matter how productive and well-intentioned we may be, we will always be vulnerable to that which is uncontrollable and unpredictable. Circumstances beyond our control may appear when we least expect them and tamper with even our most perfect plan. Our control only goes so far. Extenuating circumstances happen.

That is why we need to plan for the unexpected, as much as possible. We can't anticipate everything, but we anticipate some things. If we leave 22 minutes for a commute that takes 22 minutes, we are not expecting the unexpected. Scheduling down to the wire is inviting excuses into the equation. Waiting for the last minute is a set-up for failure.

Other people are depending on us, whether we want them to or not. We all are depending on each other, as we weave our lives, families and communities together. So when we do not carry our weight, the fabric gets a buckle in it. Even if we have a really legitimate excuse, it doesn't help those who are on the other end of the equation, who are affected by the situation.

The best we can do is apologize, see what we can learn, and move forward. So what can I learn? To make more realistic choices. To recognize that things take much longer than I expect them to. And to plan accordingly. If I don't make these adjustments, others will continue to share the cost of these mistakes with me.

So let's search out the demons. Take them on more earnestly. Be aware of our impact on others. Remember how short life is. Look at the big picture. Take action and do what needs to be done.

Starting

Start Before You're Ready

STEVEN PRESSFIELD

Don't prepare. Begin.

Remember, our enemy is not lack of preparation; it's not the difficulty of the project or the state of the marketplace or the emptiness of our bank account.

The enemy is *Resistance*.

The enemy is our chattering brain, which, if we give it so much as a nanosecond, will start producing excuses, alibis, transparent self-justifications, and a million reasons why we can't/shouldn't/won't do what we know we need to do.

Start before you're ready.

Good things happen when we start before we're ready. For one thing, we show *huevos*. Our blood heats up. Courage begets more courage. The gods, witnessing our boldness, look on in approval.

W. H. Murray said:

"Until one is committed, there is hesitancy, the chance to draw back, always ineffectiveness. Concerning all acts of initiative (and creation), there is one elementary truth, the ignorance of which kills countless ideas and splendid plans: that the moment one definitely commits oneself, then Providence moves too. A whole stream of events issues from the decision, raising in one's favor all manner of unforeseen incidents and meetings and material assistance which no man could have dreamed would have come his way. I have learned a deep respect for one of Goethe's couplets:
"Whatever you can do or dream you can, begin it. Boldness has genius, power and magic in it."

Begin it now.

Clarity

It's best to get clarity before you begin, but it's also best to begin before you have clarity.

In the Taking Action course that I teach online, the first step is to select something you want to work on, something that requires "Action." I recently posted some themes for participants to consider. Questions like,

"Why is this important?" and,

"What am I willing to give up?"

When I began work on this book I had a meeting with my assistant editor and my wife (also my editor) to discuss a "vision" for the book. I didn't want to just write another book on getting things done. I didn't want a book filled with systems for making lists and designating priorities. My vision was for a book that would draw on Eastern wisdom and would be both inspirational and practical. Something that would be a collage of quotes, anecdotes, essays and more. Just one hour of reflecting, brainstorming and talking with others helped me to envision what this book might look like. It's easier to work towards something that has a clear vision attached to it. It's easier to stay on track.

But sometimes you can't get clarity, even if you try. You have some general idea of something you want to do. Maybe it's a change of jobs, or some kind of volunteer work. Maybe you want to do something creative, but you're not sure what. Maybe you want your family to have a "nature experience" but you don't know what that means or what it would involve. So clarity isn't really available to you. What should you do?

Go ahead and get started. Get started without clarity. Take some small steps. Investigate, research, look into possibilities, check things out, talk to people, and . . . . if at all possible – try something out in real life. Be like a cook who needs to make a stew, but doesn't know what she's trying to make. Just start cooking and tasting, cooking and tasting. Add a little more pepper, or a few more carrots. "OK, this isn't quite what I was looking for. What can I add to make it different?" Worst case scenario – throw it into the compost and start over. Be willing to fail. And learn.

The problem is most of us associate figuring things out with thinking. We imagine Einstein at his blackboard, spending days writing complex equations. This may work for you if you're a physicist or mathematician. But in real life, it just keeps us stuck. It keeps us from moving forward and taking action.

Action isn't something that comes after figuring things out. Action is a way of figuring things out.

So be clear and take the next step. Or be confused and take the next step. Even if you have clarity, eventually you'll run into something that completely confuses you. And if you're confused . . you may always be confused. Life is confusing. Don't let that bother you.

Procrastination Disguised as Busyness

The meditation teacher Eknath Easwaran talks about how people have energy only when it comes to things they like. If you enjoy painting, or playing music, or a good novel, you can get lost in what you're doing and stay up for hours doing it. But if you have the opposite reaction to a task — if you don't like it — then even a five-minute phone call or ten minutes to write a letter seems like an insurmountable challenge. So we do everything we can to avoid these tasks.

One strategy is to avoid what you need to do and then spend lots of energy trying to find out why you are avoiding it. This is a great way to continue to avoid taking action. Another strategy is to assume you need to feel like doing something before you do it. Until you feel comfortable or motivated, you assume that it is not possible to move forward and take action. Actually, many people just assume that if the prospect of some task creates discomfort, they simply cannot do it.

But a popular procrastination strategy is to do something else instead. If what needs to be done is income tax preparation, then it must be time to clean the refrigerator. If what needs to be done is to work on an unfinished novel, then it must be time to pay bills. We keep busy, convincing ourselves that we are productive and hard working. Our failure to do what is important is disguised as busyness.

Here's Easwaran's comment on this:

"In India we call this "painting the bullock cart wheels." Just when the harvest is ready to be brought in, the farmer notices that the wheels of his bullock cart are looking rather shabby. Instead of going out into the fields, he takes a day to go into town for paint, and then spends a week painting beautiful designs on the cart and wheels. When he finally gets around to harvesting the rice, he has to work twelve hours a day just to keep up."

Can you identify with this strategy? Can you see the ways that you keep busy so you can avoid doing what is really important? How do we cure ourselves of this disease?

The answer is obvious, but it cannot be found in words. You cannot post it as a message or discuss it with your therapist. You cannot read about it in a book or discover it on the Internet.

Use your time wisely. It is a gift and it is only temporary. What is it that matters? What should you be doing? Are you hiding – hiding behind the veil of busyness? If so, then show yourself. Come out into the light. Be true to the work that has been placed on your path.

The Slightest Move

One of the central principles of Morita Therapy is that we have much more control over our body (actions) than our minds (thoughts, feelings). So a distinguishing element of Morita's work is to put effort into getting the body to take action, rather than trying to manipulate our thoughts or feelings. Often, once the body is moving, there is a natural influence on our emotional state and our thoughts. For example, you may not feel like exercising. and might have thoughts like "It's too cold outside to go for a walk today." But once you are out walking, you may find that your experience is one of exhilaration. As you enjoy the feeling of the warm sunlight on your face, your thoughts change to "I wonder what they are building over there at the end of the street."

Of course, you can't always control your body, particularly if your body is medically or physically incapable of a particular action. No amount of willpower will allow me to jump six feet in the air from a standing start. Nor can a person who is paralyzed from an accident stand and walk through sheer effort. There is a gray area, however, when it comes to many health and mental health problems. Someone who is severely depressed may report that he simply "can't" get out of bed. Someone with mononucleosis may say that she really cannot walk up and down the stairs. In what situations is the body physically incapable of performing a task, and in what situations is it simply due to lack of effort or willpower?

This winter, I got a severe case of the flu. For a few days, I found that I needed an inordinate amount of rest, and I would feel exhausted even after the slightest physical effort. Once I was lying down, my body felt achy, heavy and tired and I would have the thought, "I just can't get up right now." If someone else reported this, I would probably be somewhat judgmental, thinking, "Well, you could get up if you really had to." So this was a very humbling experience for me.

As I lay in bed, I continued to experiment with my situation, and I stumbled upon a technique that I believe can be helpful when we need to get our bodies moving.

I found that the best way to get myself up was to start with small muscle movements and then gradually work with larger and larger muscles. So while lying down, I would start wiggling the end of my index finger and then gradually expand that movement to all the fingers on each hand. Then I would wiggle my toes. Then lift my left arm slightly and then both arms repeatedly. Then rotate my shoulders and maybe lift a leg. At that point I could usually swing my legs over the side of the bed or sofa and stand up. Once I was up, it was easy to take a few steps. The more I would move around, the easier it was to keep moving. We might call this *the law of momentum* — it is easier to keep going once you've started than to get started in the first place. This is often true of exercise programs, diets, public dancing, writing — almost anything. It's a bit like warming up the engine in your car before you start driving.

So the next time you find yourself stuck and immobile — whether from depression or a bout of the flu — try starting your engine with just the slightest muscle movements. It may help your body get in gear, even as your mind tells you "you can't."

Starting

Jarno Virtanen

I t's amazing that you can even develop a tendency to procrastinate about a hobby — for example, blogging. I keep saying to myself that this blog isn't so serious, which it isn't, but still I keep building up a threshold for new posts. I feel that I have to put some real effort (for which I don't usually have either the time or energy) into writing so that the entries are worthwhile. And I have a slight fear of just spouting out some half-baked ideas. Therefore I end up writing nothing, nada. Classic case of procrastination.

The sad thing about procrastination with respect to a hobby is that you develop an inner conflict. You feel bad about neglecting your hobby, but on the other hand you acknowledge that the hobby isn't that serious and that you shouldn't worry about it too much. Then you tend to procrastinate even more. After a while you end up reading emphatic articles on procrastination. The idea of reading about how to cure yourself from procrastination is very thrilling. Depending on the quality of the writing, the optimistic feeling of a better life lasts either for the first few pages or sometimes for the whole article. And what a feeling it is. I'll organize my life! I'll just start! I'll no longer procrastinate!

Yeah, right.

Once you actually have to do something, the feeling disappears and you start looking for other articles about procrastination. (Which is mostly a waste of time since they all seem to have the same message.)

But today I had a minor revelation. A key strategy in the self-help articles is that you have to manage your time by dividing tasks into a manageable size. Then prioritize and just start. But doing this the right way is usually unbearable. Your head fills up with ideas about how you might manage your tasks and actions, and suddenly you feel that this process of managing your time is itself such a huge challenge that you can't handle it.

Yet today I realize that the most important thing in dividing tasks is the psychological effect of making the task bearable. The idea of small tasks always felt too abstract and not at all magical. But today it had a concrete effect on me. Suddenly, the idea of starting a task didn't seem so heavy. The tasks just need to be small enough so that they feel conquerable. After that, starting is easy. So now, do you feel excited or thrilled? Well, good.

Get moving. Get started.

What do we have here?

One of the best ways to start something is to step back, look around, and say, "What do we have here?" I learned this from a Zen cook named Edward Espe Brown, author of *The Complete Tassajara Cookbook*. This is what he did before he began preparing a meal. He would look around the kitchen, in the refrigerator, in the pantry, and ask the question, "What do we have here?" This puts you in touch with the reality of your situation. It shifts your attention from your feeling state (boredom, anxiety, confusion) to the concrete reality of the circumstances surrounding your work.

Recently I decided to make a memorial bench to honor the memory of my father, Ted Krech, who died recently. I went into the garage to search for and gather the parts of an old bench that had fallen apart. I needed to see which parts were salvageable and what I would have to build from scratch. As I found each part – a section of the metal frame, a wooden slat – I inspected it and silently asked the question, "What do we have here?"

"This piece of wood is four feet long and rotted at the ends".

"This section of metal frame has some rust on it".

"This is an unusual kind of bolt that was used to fasten the wood to the frame. Very rusty."

I leaned the pieces against a big wooden panel. I stepped back and just looked. "What do we have here?" This is what we start with. This is what we have to work with. This is what the reality of the situation is right now. Step back. Take stock. Examine. Assess.

This is where you begin.

Show Up

"Be there physically... location means
everything."
- Patricia Ryan Madson

One of the simplest approaches to taking action is to get your body in the right position. This is incredibly effective for me when it comes to writing, exercise and household repairs. Your commitment is just to be there. You're not committing to doing anything. If you do something, fine. If you don't, fine. Authors Levinson and Greider (Following Through) call *this Leading the Horse to Water*. They point out that even a thirsty horse won't drink if they're not near water.

Imagine that you need to organize your photos, but you've been putting it off for years. Now there's a family reunion approaching and you'd really like to have the photos organized in time. But it's such an overwhelming project that you can't seem to jump into action... so nothing is happening. Pick a time when you agree to just sit down with your photos and your photo album. And then just sit down. Don't plan on doing any of the sorting and organizing—just sit down and be aware of your photos. As you sit there you may take some action (organize 3-4 photos) or you can just relax for a few minutes and then put everything away. Your discipline is in showing up which takes a lot less discipline than working on your project for three hours after dinner.

"If the horse is right there where the water is, he'll certainly be more likely to drink when he does get the slightest bit thirsty. In other words, leading the horse to water puts the horse in a better position to drink."

- Levinson and Greider

Some tasks require that you show up in uniform. On Wednesday nights I show up at the gym with my shoes, ball and basketball shorts. If you're a runner, show up at your doorstep in your running outfit. If you have a household repair to make, show up with your tools.

You may end up taking action for five minutes—you might run a few hundred yards or put three photos in an album. But even if that's all you do, at least you are moving in the right direction. There's also the possibility that you will invest a bit of effort in your project once you get started. This happens to me when I work on my income tax return. I don't do it all in one sitting, but I often do more than I planned to do. That's because the suffering caused by anticipation is worse than the actual reality. We actually create more suffering for ourselves by procrastinating than we would if we just jumped into what we need to do.

Working on your tax return may not be fun, but it's not quite as bad as you expected it would be. So rather than trying to motivate yourself, psyche yourself up or work with thoughts and affirmations, just put your body in the right place at the right time. Then see what happens.

The Way of Action

Resolutions and Inspiration

If you've spent time studying yourself, you've probably come to the realization that your mind and body are on different tracks. Your mind lives in the world of thoughts – your body lives in . . . well . . . the real world. Sometimes you have a thought (*I'll go make myself a fresh cup of coffee*) and your body responds. But more often than not, you have thoughts (*I'm going to exercise tonight as soon as I get home from work*) and your body doesn't pay any attention to those thoughts. Though you may lament this condition, it's actually a good thing. If your body responded to every thought you had, your life would be in a state of complete chaos (yes, more than it is now) and you would probably be in jail.

The Zen master Kosho Uchiyama referred to our thoughts simply as "secretions."

One big difference between the thought-world and the real-world is the degree of control we have. This was one of the great insights of Japanese psychiatrist Shoma Morita (Morita

Therapy). We actually have very little control over our thoughts. Thoughts arise. They dissolve. Other thoughts arise and dissolve. In the course of our normal day, it is very unusual to "will" ourselves to have a particular thought. Good ideas, worries, likes, dislikes, criticisms of others, frustrating thoughts, thoughts about the past – they mostly arise spontaneously. On the other hand, we have much more control over our behavior. We can will ourselves to remain silent during a presentation, pick up the phone and make a call, answer an email, or drive to the store.

Another difference between the worlds of thought and action involves effort. The world of thought is a world of little effort. It doesn't take much effort to sit on the couch and think about renovating your basement. But the real world often requires lots of effort (i.e. actually renovating your basement). There are times when you're trying to figure out a complicated problem and you might have a clear sense of effort. You may feel mentally exhausted after a day of writing or taking exams. But for the most part your mind lives in a lazy world where it can think anything it wants to because it doesn't have to act. Your body, on the other hand, has to be very discriminating about what it does because just about everything requires energy and that's a precious commodity for your body.

The point of all this is that resolutions are thoughts -- they reside in the world of thought.

Most of the time, and we know this statistically, your body isn't going to listen to them. That's why most resolutions are never realized in the real world, at least for any length of time. Your body ignores them. One of the reasons your body ignores your mind is because your body is a creature of habit. It tends to do what it is already accustomed to doing.

Since we're not trying to prevent thoughts (after all, some of them might end up being brilliant) one alternative is to put your energy into *presence* – practicing mindfulness in what you're doing now. Resolutions are thoughts about what you want to do in the future. Mindfulness is about staying connected to what's real in the present. However, be careful about making mindfulness into a resolution. "I resolve to be more mindful when I eat or wash the dishes." Your mind likes to play these kind of games. It's one of the ways it finds itself amusing.

Another option is to make some changes by doing things differently. This is less about resolutions, plans and goals, and more about action. It means spending less time in the world of thought and more time in the real world, using your body to take action.

I once heard a social activist making a presentation, and during the discussion period that followed a member of the audience commented that she found the presenter's work inspiring. The

105

presenter responded by asking the audience member what she was inspired to do. There was a long pause. The presenter used that moment as an opportunity to encourage her audience to be inspired to act – not just to feel or think.

Is there something or somebody that inspires you?

To do what?

Small Steps and the Law of Momentum

"It does not matter how slowly you go, as long as you do not stop."

-- *Confucius*

A small step doesn't get you very far, and generally we judge the value of the step based on distance. If your workout today consisted of jumping rope one time (one revolution), you probably didn't burn many calories or lose much weight. On that basis we tend to discount small steps. We want to take giant steps that allow us to move forward quickly in large leaps. With a Dorothyesque click of the heels we hope to get from here to there, even when "there" is nowhere in sight. The true value of small steps is often ignored. They involve motion. We go from not doing something to doing it – even in a minimal way. According to the laws of physics, we go from being a body at rest to a body in motion.

Here's Newton's First Law of Physics:

An object at rest stays at rest and an object in motion stays in motion with the same speed and in the same direction unless acted upon by some outside force.

Sir Isaac Newton was one of the most extraordinary intellects of his time. He realized that when an object is at rest it will basically stay at rest unless something influences it. It's also true that when an object is in motion it will basically stay in motion. This is what we refer to as *momentum*. This is why small steps can be so valuable. They offer momentum at a fairly low cost. In other words, it takes very little effort to create momentum. One pushup, one dish washed, one photo organized, one paragraph written in your novel-to-be. Have you gone very far? No. Do you now have momentum? Yes! And once you have momentum (you are in motion), you are more likely to continue – in motion.

Several years ago our journal, *Thirty Thousand Days,* interviewed Dr. Robert Maurer, who wrote a book on *Kaizen.* Kaizen is a program of organizational change originally developed in Japan by an American – W. Edwards Deming. (I discuss Kaizen in the section of this book on Japanese Psychology). Maurer found that some of the same principles used in business were successful from the standpoint of personal change. When we asked him for a personal example, he mentioned writing his book. He received a contract to write a book, and felt overwhelmed. He had read that many Nobel Prize winners wrote books by committing to write one page per day. So Maurer made a commitment to write for *one minute a day*. One minute! He found that often, after one minute was up, he kept on writing – for five more minutes. Or ten. Or forty. That's how he wrote a book. He used Newton's First Law of Physics. He created momentum – and he finished his book.

Momentum doesn't guarantee you will remain in motion. There will always be forces working against you – internal forces (like anxiety or fear) and external forces (like emergency medical problems and illness). You can do something every day for a month and then miss a day. Are you back at square one? Yes and No. You have to start over again and get back in motion. But you're not the same person you were a month ago. You have different karma. You have a different history.

Once you understand momentum, you can get it to work in your favor. And when you become aware that you have become a "body at rest," you realize that you will also remain that way unless something changes. How to take that first step from being a "body at rest" to being a "body in motion" is something you have to learn to do. While you're trying to figure it out, go ahead and do it.

The Turtles Are On the Move

L ast week I saw a painted turtle on the road not far from our driveway. We found another in our garden the next day. A few years ago, we actually found one on our deck underneath the picnic table. June is the month when turtles are on the move here in Vermont. This is their month for taking action. They are slow creatures on land, and if you watch them crawl through a yard, you see how painstakingly slow their steps are. Except for the largest turtles, a single step doesn't get them very far – only a few inches. But in June, they leave the comfort of the ponds and streams to find nesting sites – often in sunny areas with loose soil where they can dig a hole and deposit their eggs. We've actually watched one along our driveway in the process of laying eggs. Amazing!

These turtles are an inspiration to me. They're not fast or strong or even particularly smart. They leave their comfort zone and put themselves in danger. But they have a clear purpose. And they are not to be deterred. Sometimes people find them on the road and move them back to the side of the road closest to the water. But the turtles know where they're going, and they will simply turn around and go back in the opposite direction. These turtles can teach us about persistence, purpose and effort. Generally, I consider myself "superior" to a turtle. I'll see them basking in the sun on logs when I'm kayaking and think, "Boy, what an easy life." But in June, when I witness their determination and notice what these small, slow creatures are able to accomplish, I am truly humbled. I think, "Wow, I wish I could be like that!"

Likes and Dislikes

"Never mind likes and dislikes; they are of no consequence.
Just do what must be done.
This may not be happiness, but it is greatness."

— *GEORGE BERNARD SHAW*

We tend to do what we like to do and the things we are comfortable doing. We gravitate towards activities that we expect will give us pleasure. On the other hand, we tend to avoid tasks that . . .

- Stimulate feelings of discomfort

- Stimulate feelings of fear and anxiety

- We simply don't enjoy doing

- Have no clear solution or sequence of steps

- Seem overwhelming

- Have no immediate reward

- Have been difficult or problematic in the past

Over time we develop, or are conditioned to have, "likes and dislikes." This assortment of likes and dislikes becomes the basis for some of the greatest practical and spiritual challenges of our lives.

Eknath Easwaran, the meditation teacher, says,

"Nothing in life is more satisfying, more masterful, than to be able to change our likes and dislikes when we need to. In fact, anyone who has mastered this skill has mastered life, and anyone who has not learned to overcome likes and dislikes is a victim of life. The statement we hear so often these days – 'I like it, so I'm going to do it' -- is a confession that a person is not free. When I say, 'I am going to do this because I like it; I am not going to do that because I don't like it,' what I am really saying is, 'My hands are bound; I have no choice in life.'"

I'd like to expand a bit on the issue of putting off things which don't have a clear solution or sequence of steps. A classic example of this is repairs. Something stops working and we think, "Oh, my. What's wrong with it?" In some cases, we just bring it into a repair shop. Or we call a repair person to come out and fix it. But some of us try to fix things ourselves. In many cases, there's no clear solution . . . at least not initially. So we have to treat the situation as a mystery. Have you ever read a good mystery, or watched a mystery/suspense film? They can be very exciting. Generally there's a character who is trying to solve the mystery. At the moment, I'm thinking of *The Da Vinci Code*, a murder mystery with a very suspenseful and elaborate plot. So there are several characters who are trying to solve the mystery. What do they do?

They INVESTIGATE.

This is how you can approach repairs – as a mystery. You can investigate. To investigate you have to examine things physically. You take it apart. You try to figure out how it actually works. You ask questions. You look at it from different angles. At this point, you don't know how to actually solve the problem. You're just trying to understand what's going on.

Mostly, we don't try to understand others, because we're preoccupied with other people understanding us. So this is an experience where we have to just immerse ourselves in curiosity. We have to abandon our self-preoccupation and just try to understand something outside of ourselves. If you have a job as an investigator (an auto repair person, computer tech, doctor, electrician, etc.), you are in the habit of investigating mysteries. But if you don't have that type of job, or, if the mystery is in a field you are unfamiliar with, then there is often a natural inclination to shift our effort to what we do know. We clean the house, wash the dishes, mow the lawn, pull weeds in the garden, or sew on a button. There are clear, straightforward steps to accomplishing these tasks.

We don't need to investigate to determine how to solve the problem.

In truth, tasks such as weeding or sewing can involve profound levels of investigation, if we really approached them with a "beginner's mind." Mundane chores can reveal great mysteries.

So we gravitate towards what is clear and away from what is mysterious. We gravitate towards what is known and away from what is unknown. We abandon curiosity and investigation in order to rest comfortably in our perceived sense of certainty.

Try investigating something today. Be curious. Stretch yourself. Take on a problem for which the answer is shrouded in mystery. Don't just think about it – actually investigate it.

Be the Lewis and Clark of broken coffeemakers, or the Jonas Salk of setting up a new website. Exploration brings excitement as well as anxiety. They are really two sides of the same coin. Don't let the expedition leave without you. Venture into the unknown.

Notice your likes and dislikes and learn to do what you don't like. And if you're not sure what action to take, be curious . . . and investigate.

Working with the Conditions We Encounter

J anet Lipner had a realization recently. She attended a tree care program and, after getting certified, she helped to plant trees. She commented on all the factors that help a tree grow: depth and circumference of the hole, soil quality, water, etc. But wherever you plant the tree, the tree has to deal with whatever conditions are present in that location. This is really true of any kind of plant, since they cannot move or change their circumstances. But the tree doesn't complain about its situation saying,

"I should have been planted in a better spot; now I can't grow well."

The tree does its best with what it gets. It's easy for us to focus on how we were dealt a lousy hand in life and use that as a constant source of complaint and excuse as to why we haven't done better. This type of attitude contributes to our own suffering and to the suffering of others. In fact, by complaining like this we create conditions for the "trees" around us that make their lives more difficult. So perhaps we can take a lesson from our friends, the trees, and simply do our best with whatever situation we encounter. The conditions of our lives will always be less than ideal. But just to be planted on this earth for the short period of time we call 'this life' is truly a gift that we should continuously reflect on.

"I recently found an old journal with an embarrassing entry detailing the conditions I thought I needed to become a writer. I would awaken each morning to Pachelbel's Canon and the aroma of freshly brewed expresso. I would stroll down an antique brick path bordered by blackspot-resistant roses to a picturesque Victorian garden cottage. Once there I would begin typing my immortal musings into a user-friendly machine while my flealess Labrador Retriever would lie adoringly at my feet. Fantasy? Sort of. But as some level I really did believe the universe owed me a better set of circumstances before I could step out on my heart's path. In reality, all I need is a ballpoint pen and the back of a dry cleaning receipt . . . and the faith to take that first step in crafting an essay or article. Now, when I need a faith-lift, I just glance down at the neon green Post-It note my Quaker friend attached to my computer. It says, 'Proceed as the path opens.' And in case I need a nudge, the action verb PROCEED is circled in scarlet."

- Victoria Register-Freeman (author, **Love Stories from the Bible**)

117

The Perils of Excitement

"Enthusiasm is often connected to something new. But, like any feeling state, it doesn't last. It fades. You used those feelings to help you get started, but now they're not available any more."

- Gregg Krech

Remember the last time you were excited in anticipation of something. Perhaps it was a long-awaited trip to some dreamed-of destination. Or expecting delivery of the first published copies of your book. Maybe you were planning a romantic weekend getaway with your lover. Or even the arrival of a new purchase — a car, computer or furniture. It's common for us to get excited in anticipation of something pleasant that is about to happen.

Sometimes we get excited as we're about to take on a project — the writing of a book, house renovations, learning a foreign language, or just about anything we believe will create happiness or satisfaction when it is accomplished.

Our excitement is related to how we think things will be once we've accomplished our goal. Unfortunately, this excitement is often a blight which leaves us in ruins with unfinished projects, abandoned goals and even failed relationships. Excitement, which we seek and think of as pleasant, can also be the cause of great distress.

It's not really the feeling of excitement itself which is the culprit here, it is the loss of excitement which then prompts us to abandon our efforts towards fulfillment of our dreams — dreams which were, at one time, very exciting to us. If anticipatory excitement moves us to action, the loss of excitement often prompts us to stop. Action dissolves into inaction.

Meditation teacher Eknath Easwaran tells us of a Sanskrit word — *arambhashura* — which means "heroes at the beginning" — people who take up a job with a fanfare of trumpets but soon find that their enthusiasm has tiptoed down the back stairs.

Why does our excitement wane over time? Because that's the way our minds work. Our minds associate "newness" with excitement and something is only new in the beginning. Over time, we become accustomed to the object, person, or environment and we cease to respond with feelings of excitement. In the course of a project, we are excited about the "idea" of the project, but most projects turn out to be more difficult and complicated than we expect them to be. And over time we may grow weary. Or confused. Or frustrated. Such feelings replace the excited feelings that we had in the beginning. This happens in relationships as well, as the romantic phase fades and we discover that a meaningful, intimate relationship requires effort, skill, patience and conflict resolution.

So what do we do when the feeling of excitement is gone? Well, many of us simply abandon what we're doing and look for something new to get excited about — a new project, a new purchase, a new partner. We change our circumstances, but we don't really address the underlying problem, so we are just getting in line to go through the entire cycle again, like a popular ride at Disneyworld.

Another option is to find ways to rekindle the feeling of excitement. We may have some temporary success, but, again, the underlying problem is still there. *The only way to really deal with the problem of excitement is to stop becoming dependent on it.* We stop connecting the feeling of excitement with the persistence of action-taking. We stay with something because it remains important, even *after* our excited feelings are gone.

So the next time you are about to start something important, enjoy the excitement that may accompany you on the initial steps of your journey. Start off singing and dancing as you head down the yellow brick road towards the emerald city of Oz. But remember that it won't be long until your excitement fades and you meet frustration, tedium and even doubt. This is where you remind yourself of your purpose. This is where you reach deep down and find the jewel of your determination. This is where you discover the ability to face life's challenges without the training wheels of newness and excitement. There is great potential in this formula for making dreams into reality.

It's all very exciting, isn't it?

Swimming Upstream

JULIE GUROFF

The clear river flows, slides, splashes and rolls downstream

rushing between rocks that funnel the water into narrow passages

curling into quiet eddies that reflect sky, clouds, and brilliant sun.

On a pale spring day the silver-sided fish swim upstream

fulfilling their assignment to perpetuate their lives.

Look carefully. See how the current sometimes ruffles the fins of their backs as they swim.

Do the fish feel a delicious thrill up and down their backbones as the ends of the little fin bones flutter against their vertebrae?

Fish don't move at a steady speed.

A tiny sideways bend and snap of their bodies kicks them forward.

Then they coast almost to a stop against the push of the water before they flip forward again.

The cycle of effort and rest, effort and rest.

Working with the water's changing force, they move along the constantly shifting shape of the river bed.

Do they enjoy the variations, like a cross-country runner weaving among the hills?

Upstream, in a stretch of white feathered riffles, you can see the fish jumping over wavelets, their bodies curving and shining in the sun.

Gathered in the rocks are small quiet eddy pools that attract a steady supply of tasty bugs.

A few fish pause in a pool, just below the water's surface, and sample the buffet.

Is it hard work swimming upstream? Probably.

Do the fish moan about how the current holds them back

how they just can't seem to get anything done

how staying mindful enough to overcome the pressure is nearly impossible?

Apparently not.

Swimming upstream is the true nature of the fish.

They accept the ever-changing current as it is, and they swim elegantly through it and against it.

People, though, are not always so graceful.

We tend to complain and try to escape the counter-pressure we meet in the course of doing what needs doing.

There's the cantankerous co-worker who creates difficulty

or the urgent medical expense that costs the price of what we wanted to buy.

And there's the pressure from within –

fear of failure, wandering of attention, anxiety,

or the dull ache that goes with knowing that we've postponed and avoided that which needed our attention.

Sometimes we give up and are swept downstream to the next distraction.

The endless flow of thoughts, feelings and outside circumstances pressing against us, as if determined to hold us back.

Yet, sometimes, people welcome pressure against their efforts, calling it training or practice.

There's even a company that advertises a swimming pool with a built-in pump to generate current for its affluent owner to swim against!

Why limit ourselves to such contrivances in order to develop talent, strength and grace under pressure?

The source of the natural current we're trying to move through is upstream - exactly where we want to go.

Can we accept the natural, ever-changing current of life's river as it is?

Can we swim elegantly and effortfully through the current, against the current

forgetting the current (and ourselves) as we discover moments of joy from time to time?

Relaxing into the swimming. Relaxing into the cycle – effort and rest

effort and rest.

"I Get To"

KATE MANAHAN

Do you ever have to interrupt what you are focused on to go pick your kids up at school? Do you ever put dinner together for the family because you should, not because you are inspired to do so? If you regularly use the phrase "I have to" or "I should" in your life, perhaps you will enjoy this exercise a friend recently shared with me.

Any time you begin to say "I should" or "I have to," try replacing it with "I get to."

This simple word substitution prompts a far different mindset. "I have to go pick up the kids" becomes "I get to go pick up the kids." Consider what that means: I get the chance to check in with some of their teachers. I get to say hello to friends in the parking lot. I get to see my children's rapt faces filled with all the stories of the day. I get to enter the beautiful building taxpayers have created for families just like mine. How fortunate I am to get to have kids. With a turn of phrase I can notice a Naikan-like sense of appreciation shift the balance in my everyday life.

As six o'clock rolled around, my thoughts would sometimes sound something like, "Uh, I guess I should make something for dinner tonight."

Now, when I catch myself and substitute "I get to," I suddenly see how every cupboard has food in it. The refrigerator has fresh vegetables picked by stooped farmers. Truckers, away from their families, deliver fresh food to our market. There are about 50 varieties of such produce to choose from every time I go to the local grocery store.

The process is transformative. I get to make choices: spaghetti or tacos. It is not gruel or rice, day in and out. I get to have a hand in promoting my children's nutrition and growth. I get to turn on the stove and have instant heat. I get to put a clean pan on the stove to make our meal. Before I know it, I am half done with the dinner preparation and in a far finer state of mind. I feel grateful for the myriad blessings in our day-to-day lives.

I laugh to myself at how this simple turn of phrase has changed my thinking. I get to floss my teeth. I get to take my car in to be repaired. I get to help my sons find a workable solution to their conflicts. Using "I get to" allows me to see that my daily deeds are gifts. Life is burgeoning with opportunities to meet our human needs. In context, it is all a blessing. I finally get to see that.

What might you "get to" do today?

Forgotten Shovel

Once, everybody at the Tassajara Zen Center took some tools and climbed a long hot dusty mountain trail to work on some project. When they reached the top of the mountain they discovered that they had forgotten the shovel and began discussion about who should return and get it. After the discussion had ended they realized that Roshi (Shunryu Suzuki) wasn't there. He was already half-way down the mountain trail, on his way back to pick up the shovel.

Not So Fast

Slowing down could be the single most effective action to save the world

DONELLA MEADOWS

Those of us who think the world needs saving — from environmental destruction, rapacious greed, decaying morals, drugs, crime, racism, whatever — keep very busy crusading for our favorite remedies. School vouchers. Carbon taxes. Campaign reform. The Endangered Species Act. A lower capital gains tax. Strong regulation. No regulation. You know, that long list of mutually inconsistent Holy Grails with which we like to hit each other over the head.

There's one solution to the world's problems, however, that I never hear the frenzied activists suggest.

Slowing down.

Slowing down could be the single most effective solution to the particular save-the-world struggle I immerse myself in — the struggle for sustainability, for living harmoniously and well within the limits and laws of the Earth.

Suppose we weren't in such a hurry. We could take time to walk instead of drive, to sail instead of fly. To clean up our messes. To discuss

129

our plans throughout the whole community before we send in bulldozers to make irreversible changes. To figure out how many fish the ocean can produce before boats race out to beat other boats to whatever fish are left.

Suppose we went at a slow enough pace not only to smell the flowers, but to feel our bodies, play with children, look openly without agenda or timetable into the faces of loved ones. Suppose we stopped gulping fast food and started savoring slow food, grown, cooked, served and eaten with care. Suppose we took time each day to sit in silence.

I think, if we did those things, the world wouldn't need much saving. We could cut our energy and material use drastically, because we would get the full good out of what we use. We wouldn't have to buy so many things to save time. (Have you ever wondered, with all our time-saving paraphernalia, what happens to the time we save?) We wouldn't make so many mistakes. We could listen more and hurt each other less. Maybe we could even take time to reason through our favorite solutions, test them, and learn what their actual effects are.

According to Thomas Merton, who spent his time in a Trappist monastery, *"There is a pervasive form of contemporary violence to which the idealist . . . most easily succumbs: activism and over-work... To allow oneself to be carried away by a multitude of conflicting concerns, to surrender to too many demands, to commit oneself to too many people, to want to help everyone in everything, is to succumb to violence. The frenzy of the activist neutralizes his work for peace. It destroys the fruitfulness of his own work, because it kills the root of inner wisdom which makes work fruitful."*

A friend in India tells me that the onslaught of Western advertising in his country is a cultural blow, not so much because of the messages of the ads but because of their pace. The stun-the-senses barrage of all TV programming, especially ads, is antithetical to a thousands-year-old tradition of contemplation. I can imagine that. I have been driven crazy by the somnolent pace at which things get done in India. Don't these people know that time is money? What they know, actually, is that time is life, and to go zooming through it is to miss living.

Slow... d o w n. Do that first. Then, quietly, carefully, think about what else might need to be done.

The only problem with this cure is that I can't prescribe it for others, because I have such trouble following it myself. It's so easy to get swept up in the hurtling pace of the world. Like most of the other world-savers I know, I'm way too busy to eat well, sit quietly, take a vacation, or even, some days, think.

Slow down. Good advice. Too bad I don't have time to take it. I have to go save the world.

The Rhythm of Your Activity

"There is rhythm in everything."
- Miyamoto Musashi*

Many songs introduce you to the rhythm before the lyrics or melody. So in the beginning of the song, you may simply be aware of the rhythm. I used to have a small personal recording studio, and when recording a song, the first thing you do is establish the rhythm. You might record a metronome beat or a "drum track" and that would be the foundation of the song's timing. If you dance to music, you're generally not dancing to the melody or lyrics, you're dancing to the beat or the rhythm. If the tone of that rhythm is deep, like a bass guitar or a bass drum, your body can actually feel the vibrations. Because your body tunes into the rhythmic vibrations, you don't even have to think about the music. Your body just moves in sync with the rhythm.

Many people have a basic rhythm to their day, or at least their morning. The rhythm isn't really about what's being done (brushing teeth, making coffee), it's the pace and timing of how it's done. Think about your morning rhythm. Do you start out very slow and then speed up in the last ten minutes because you realize you are running late? Do you have a relatively even pace from the time you get out of bed until the time you get in your car to leave for work? What about your kids? How would you describe their pace/timing on a weekday morning as they prepare for school?

Even within a particular morning, there is a rhythm to our specific activities. For example, I have a rhythm to making coffee in the morning. There is also a rhythm to the speed with which I walk through the house. There is a rhythm to my riding a bike and to putting the groceries away. You may not be aware of your rhythm as you move from activity to activity, but it's there.

"The rhythm with which things progress, and
the rhythm with which things deteriorate
should be understood and differentiated."
- Miyamoto Musashi

Prior to my sophomore year of college I worked at a UPS distribution center in Northbrook, Illinois. My job was to load packages on to the UPS trucks -- not the delivery trucks that come to your house, but the long semi-trailers that you see on the interstate. In the distribution center there were literally miles of assembly line belts that delivered the packages right into the front of these trailers once they were sorted by zip code. I would be assigned to a particular truck and my job was to get the packages as they came off the belt and then carry them towards the back of the truck where I would stack them in a tight wall so they could be transported without damage. We had been taught a particular strategy for loading the trucks and to do it correctly we had to be attentive to the proper way of stacking the packages. The challenge was that the speed in which packages arrived off the belt varied tremendously. Sometimes a box would come and I would pick up the box, walk to the back of the truck, and carefully consider the best spot for it according to my design strategy. Then I would walk back to the end of the belt and watch as another package came towards me. But often, without warning, the packages would start coming closer together, and by the time I had stacked one package, there were 2-3 more already in the truck waiting for me. So you can probably guess what I had to do. I had to speed up. I had to adjust my rhythm to meet the rhythm of the incoming work.

Perhaps you've had this experience in your life. You find yourself in a situation where the packages are coming at you very fast. It feels overwhelming. So you speed up to try to meet the demands you're faced with. That's fine. The problem is that you may develop a fast rhythm and start to apply that to every situation in your life. But not all situations call for a fast rhythm. I recently read a story about a father who was nearly always worked at a fast pace in his workplace. In the evening, he had trouble slowing down and relaxing, even when there was no time pressure. He would put his two year old son to bed and every night he would read him a bedtime story. But he became very impatient with the pace of the story, so he would speed up his reading, even if it meant his son couldn't quite follow the story. One day he heard about a book called, "Sixty Second Bedtime Stories" and he thought, "This is great." Now he could get through the story in just one minute. Fortunately, a light bulb went off for him. "Wait a minute. This is a special time for my son and me. Why am I trying to rush through it?"

The problem is that we can develop a habitual rhythm, and then it becomes difficult for us to adjust our rhythm to the needs of the situation. My initial training in Zen was at a Rinzai Zen temple in Japan. We did walking meditation in between the periods of sitting meditation. We walked in a circle very fast – almost running. That was the style I was taught in that type of Zen training. A few years later I was training with Thich Nhat Hanh, a Vietnamese Zen teacher. He also taught walking meditation, but he taught us to do it slowly. Verrrrrrry Sloooooowly. This felt extremely awkward at first and I found it hard to concentrate and adapt to this style. It took a while before it felt somewhat comfortable.

The key is to be able to adjust our rhythm to the needs of the situation. If we are packing in the morning to catch a flight we may need a rather quick pace. If we are reading a bedtime story to our daughter, perhaps a rather slow, relaxed pace is more enjoyable. There is no ideal rhythm for our life, just as there's no ideal rhythm for music.

There's one "glitch" to this principle. You may have noticed that it's generally easier to keep your attention focused on what you're doing when you are doing it at a "moderate" rhythm. If we go too fast, we tend to lose our focus and our mind races ahead of our body. But if we go too slow, we can find that the mind begins incessant chattering about things that have nothing to do with what we're doing -- so we also lose focus. This doesn't mean we should try to work at a moderate pace. It simply means that we need to stay focused on the present, regardless of our rhythm. Whether you're dancing a tango, a fox trot or the Texas two-step, keep your attention on what's happening in the present moment. Then you can enjoy bedtime stories as well as the chaos of getting your kids off to school.

From our perspective it's easy to see the rhythm of the seasons or the rhythm of the day and night. From the perspective of the Universe (i.e.

God/Buddha), we are a beat in a much larger rhythm. Our life is a single beat on the bass drum or a single crash of a cymbal. It's a timeless rhythm. So make sure you come in on time. And make some noise when you do!

Miyamoto Musashi (1584-1645) was a master swordsman and samurai. He is the author of The Book of Five Rings – a book on strategy and philosophy of the swordsman.

Overcoming by Going Around

The other day I was walking down our driveway which had become icy as a result of sleet, freezing rain, a warm sun, and then cold frigid temperatures. One large segment of the driveway was like a skating rink. Even if you walked very carefully, it was almost impossible to cross the ice without slipping and falling. So I decided to simply go around the ice by walking alongside the driveway where there were still several inches of crusty, hard snow. By going around the ice, I was able to continue my walk without confronting the ice directly.

This is the strategy Morita therapy offers for dealing with the challenging feeling-states we all face from time to time -- depression, fear, anxiety, despair, frustration and even anger. We are generally taught that we must face our problems and confront them directly. This can work well when the problem is a car that won't start or weeds in your garden. You get in there and work hard on the problem until it is solved. But this doesn't work very well when the "problem" is our feeling state. For this problem, we are better off learning how to "overcome by going around."

"There is an old Buddhist term, ocho, which means overcoming by going around. In confronting a problem head-on, you may encounter a wall so high and thick that you cannot break through it. So you turn to one side and go around the wall. This is ocho. Instead of sitting desolately in front of the wall that is blocking your progress, you try to get around it by making a long detour, or even by digging under it… It is a subtle but simple movement of the mind that makes this transformation complete, but an invaluable one to learn and perfect."
— Hiroyuki Itsuki

It takes a lot of strength to knock down a wall of depression. It takes great courage to break through a wall of fear. But to simply go around the wall doesn't require any strength or courage at all. It requires a bit of wisdom. It requires clarity of purpose. And it requires acceptance. We leave the ice intact. We leave the wall standing.

I saw a wonderful example of this applied by a musician who had stage fright. He wanted to perform in front of an audience. But when he did, he was terrified. And his voice would shake which affected his singing. Do you know how he conquered his stage fright? He wrote a song about it. And when he performed he would sing that song. He said the greater his anxiety, the more his voice would shake, and that actually improved his song. It made the performance better. Instead of doing battle with his anxiety, he found a way to make it work for him.

We overcome our anxiety by going around it, not by destroying it or freeing ourselves from it. You don't need to travel in a straight line. Water doesn't travel in a straight line. Because of its flexibility it is impossible to contain it. Let us learn the art of *ocho* and live more like water.

Taking Action in the Midst of Sadness

"Hold the sadness and pain of samsara in your heart and at the same time the power and vision of the Great Eastern Sun. Then the warrior can make a proper cup of tea."
- Chogyam Trungpa

The great Tibetan Buddhist teacher, Chogyam Trungpa, gave a talk which provides excellent advice on how to move forward in life even though our hearts might be filled with sadness. His guidance is:

"Hold the sadness and pain of samsara in your heart and at the same time the power and vision of the Great Eastern Sun. Then the warrior can make a proper cup of tea."

The first thing we must do is be willing to hold our pain and sadness in our heart. Most of us do this, but not skillfully enough. We are in touch with the disappointment of not getting a promotion, the frustration of our child's drug addiction, or even the gloom that comes from watching the news of all the violence and harm being done in the world. But to hold the sadness and pain in our heart is to be aware of the sadness

141

and pain in our heart. We notice and acknowledge the feeling of disappointment, gloom, and frustration -- and we hold it in our heart with warmth and tenderness. Think about how you usually respond to the feeling of sadness or depression. You want to get rid of it. You want to avoid it. You want to make it go away. This is usually why people go to therapy. We want to fix our feelings. That is different than holding our experience in our heart. We meet our sadness with tenderness. We meet our pain with warmth and openness.

The second element of Trungpa's advice is to hold the power and vision of the Great Eastern Sun in our heart at the same time. Now this is tricky. What is the Great Eastern Sun, anyway? The Great Eastern Sun represents a combination of wisdom and discipline. It is about moving forward. It is about waking up to your life. The Great Eastern Sun shows us what to do and not do. It is cheerful, illuminating and carries the quality of nonaggression. So we are asked to hold on to this vision and experience even as we hold on to our sadness and pain. Is this possible? Can we hold two seemingly opposing views in our heart simultaneously? Try it and see if you can do it.

This morning I sat on the deck of the ToDo Institute, staring out at a beautiful valley that was bathed in the morning sun, revealing the hillsides of the rolling Green Mountains. In the background was the sound of bluejays, chickadees and crows. Red squirrels were chattering in the tall pine above me. There was a gentle breeze coming from the west and the petunia petals were dancing ever so slightly. Yet I am sad. My 83 year-old mother was diagnosed with cancer last week. She lives seven hundred miles away and this morning she is in a nursing facility. She is depressed and lonely. She is refusing treatment and says she wants to die. So I am holding this great sadness in my heart while I am bathing in the morning sun, the songs of the birds and the joy of being surrounded by a wonderful family of my own. I am aware of the impermanence of life and that all things must change. And at the same time I am filled with the pain of my mother's suffering.

The haiku poet Issa represents this beautifully in one of his most famous poems:

The world of dew

Is the world of dew.

And yet, and yet …

He wrote this poem after the funeral of his baby daughter. All three of his children died before they reached their first birthday. What great sadness he had to carry in his heart. He understands that this world is impermanent. The "world of dew" is a world of birth and death. The morning dew is here in the morning and gone once it meets the rays of the sun. All things are subject to change. So Issa's recognition of "the world of dew" is a statement of his own realization. He understands the way the world is. But "and yet, and yet" is a statement of his pain. It is the cry of a human being. It reflects his own humanity as a father. In this very short poem, he expresses both his sadness and his wisdom. In this moment he appears to hold both his pain and the Great Eastern Sun in his tender heart.

There is one final step in Trungpa's advice: make a proper cup of tea. Up to this point, everything is about meditation and contemplation. But Trungpa wants us to take action. He wants us to get up and live our life. What is there to do? Make a cup of tea? Feed the birds? Plan a trip to visit your mother or write a letter to your Senator? Our heart is filled with both sadness and joy. And we take that heart with us as we act. We move forward with our life and with the awareness that our life (everyone's life) is a bundle of pain and joy.

Pema Chodron, a Buddhist teacher and former student of Chogyam Trungpa, adds a cautionary note to his quote. She says,

"You can be willing to feel fully and acknowledge continually your own sadness and the sadness of life, but at the same time not be drowned in it."

This is the difficulty many of us have when acknowledging our own pain and suffering. We are drowned by it. We lose sight of the Great Eastern Sun and we either take no action, or we act from a heart which is consumed by sadness and depression.

We have a great challenge to meet today. We have to acknowledge our sadness, but also acknowledge the joy, care and blessings of our life. We have to feel our pain but not be drowned by it. We have to take our sad and joyful heart with us and live our life and do what is important for us to do. That's asking a lot, isn't it?

Yes, it is.

Non-attachment: Effort and Outcomes

Whenever we're facing a challenging situation, one of the wisest things we can do is take a few minutes to distinguish between what's controllable and what isn't controllable. This is one of the key elements of Morita Therapy and it's an example of how something very simple can also be very helpful. I suggest you use a pencil and paper. Simply divide the paper into two columns and, as you reflect on the situation, place each element into the proper column. What you end up with is a "map" that shows what you can work on (actions which are controllable by you) and what you can't control. This empowers you to move forward and do what you can do.

This exercise is also helpful when considering our dreams and aspirations. We live in a goal-oriented culture and we receive encouragement to identify goals, write them down, and work towards them. There's nothing inherently wrong with this, except that we can quickly find ourselves attached to the goals themselves, which are nearly always outcomes. *And outcomes, in most cases, are uncontrollable.* Finding a job, losing weight, getting a book published or finding someone for an intimate relationship are examples of outcomes which you really can't control. When these outcomes become the main focus, we implicitly define success based on accomplishing something outside our control. Sometimes we are successful, and sometimes we aren't.

The alternative is to focus on the effort we make. Our effort is almost always controllable – an action, something we can do. Let's take the example of finding a job. The outcome, of course, is getting hired. But we certainly can't control getting a job offer, no matter how hard we try or how well we present ourselves. Instead, we need to keep our focus on making the best effort possible while searching for a job. We can create a professional resume, network with others, and send lots of applications with tailored cover letters. We can make phone calls and follow-up, show up on time for interviews, and be well prepared. If we do all this, and more, will we get a good job? Not necessarily. There's still no certainty we'll get hired at all. But if we've done everything we can do, and we've done it to the best of our ability . . . that can be our measure of success.

Most of us would like the assurance that if we just work hard enough towards a goal, we'll accomplish it. But it doesn't always work that way. We have to accept the limits of our human control over the world. We have to accept the uncertainty of the way life unfolds. Attachment to our goals traps us in a life of seeking more and more control which not only creates disappointment, but creates an ongoing source of pressure and stress.

A second benefit of moving from a focus on goals to a focus on effort, is that it naturally moves us from *focusing on the future to focusing on the present*. Goals are what we desire or hope will happen in the future. Goals have a distance between our life as it is and life as we hope it will be. But our effort is what we're doing now! And when we move from the future to the present, we move from the imaginations of the mind to the grounded reality of real life. Suppose we wish to take a trip around the world. What can we do right now?

- Open a savings account.
- Investigate special round-the-world airfares.
- Research possible destinations.

Our actions are in the present moment. Our ideas about action are just thoughts about something we want to happen later.

And finally, when we are truly focused on effort, rather than outcomes, we find it easier to resist the temptation to abandon our integrity. When we're preoccupied with a particular outcome, it's natural to lose sight of our morals and values. If we have to "bend the truth a bit," that's okay because what's important is getting the outcome we want. In essence, the end justifies the means. But if our focus is on effort, then "how" we move forward is of great importance. We consider the impact of our actions on others.

We consider values such as honesty, loyalty or generosity. What does it mean to handle a situation with integrity?

So the next time you consider a goal or dream, come back to the present circumstances of your life and take a constructive step forward. Make your effort the focus of your attention. Make your effort one which is sincere, attentive, persistent and thorough. Once you've done that, leave the outcome to life (or God or Buddha). There are too many uncontrollable influences to know, with any certainty, how things will unfold. Even a strong, well-built ship can be blown off course. We have to find a way to enjoy the journey, even when we don't get the results we hoped for. Sometimes, those surprising, unhoped-for results are a real blessing.

Then we realize that life can be worthwhile without us being in control.

And that opens a new doorway . . . . to faith.

Keep Your Feet Moving

There's a story that comes from the Tibetan tradition about a young man who has been in spiritual training for several years with his teacher. He is about to embark on one of the tests of his training. He must enter a room which is pitch black, make his way through the room and find the exit door. In the room are demons, and each demon represents one of his greatest fears. As he prepares to enter his teacher offers him two pieces of advice:

"First, remember that the demons aren't real. But when you encounter them they will seem real. So you must maintain a presence of mind and know, even as you are filled with fear, that the demon is not real."

"And what is the other piece of advice, my teacher?"

"No matter what happens, keep your feet moving. If you keep your feet moving, eventually you will find the way out. But if you stop moving, your attention will be absorbed by fear and it will be hard to get your body moving again."

The student took the teacher's advice and entered the room. Horrifying demons, transforming themselves into his fears, swarmed at him and surrounded him. At times, he forgot his master's first piece of advice and thought they must be real. But he kept his feet moving. And he found the way out.

Faith in Action

SHARON SALZBERG

When someone's suffering seems to have no end, when it is too much to bear, we can lose faith in our ability to make any difference at all. But it is exactly at these times when faith is most needed. How do we cultivate a faith that enables us to take positive action in the world against even overwhelming odds? Where can we place our faith that enables us to work to make a difference — especially when it seems that no matter what we do, it's not enough?

When I'm at the ragged edge of an anxious night, when I've tried hard to help someone and am drained by frustration and grief, when the suffering I encounter threatens to pull me down into futility, I need to begin by reminding myself of what I am not seeing in the picture of suffering right before me.

For my fortieth birthday, my friend Carol gave me a small picture book. In the center of its vivid red cover was the one-word title — *Zoom* — and the author's name, I. Banyai. Curious, I opened the book and on the first page saw an abstract image of something red and pointy. The next page showed a colorful rooster, whose comb was the image I'd just seen. *This is a book with no words in it, about a rooster, I mused. How very peculiar to receive this as a gift when I'm turning forty, not four.* Carol smiled, urging me to go on. I turned the page and saw a picture of children looking through the window of a house at the rooster. *Oh, I thought, it's not a book about a rooster; it's about some children who live on a farm.*

As I turned more pages, the children and the house diminished in size until they proved to be pieces in a toy village being arranged by a little girl. *Oh, now I understand, I thought. It's a book about a child, and she is the central figure in this story; the other figures were just her toys.* A page later, the girl playing with the houses turned out to be part of an illustration on the cover of a book being held by a boy. And so on it went.

As I turned the pages, I came to conclusion after conclusion about what the book was really about. *Okay, now I get it. This is a story about a boy who is on an ocean liner holding a book with a cover picturing a child playing with a miniature village.* But when the entire ocean liner turned out to be part of a billboard posted on the side of a bus, my confidence in my interpretations collapsed.

The bus proved to be part of a scene on a TV screen being watched by a cowboy in a desert, which turned out to be the illustration on a postage stamp, which was on a postcard in the hands of a group of people standing on an island beach. Before I could try to reach another conclusion about the subject of this book, a turn of the page showed the island as seen by a pilot in a small plane. Several pages later, through swirls of clouds, I saw the earth, a jewel-like globe floating in infinite space, then simply a distant white dot. Opened to an immensity of perspective, my vision included every image in an expansive sweep of vision, but was not limited by any one of them. I looked up at Carol and said, "I feel like God!"

There is a far bigger picture to life than what we are facing in any particular moment. To see beyond the one small part in front of us and to think that's all there is, we have to look past our ready conclusions. When we see only the suffering before us and our actions in response to it, it is no wonder we might conclude that what we do seems inadequate. We may think the final result of something we've done is visible on page four of the story, or page seven. But as we turn page after page, we step outside our own limited perspective and realize that there is more to come. Both the suffering and our efforts to address it are woven into an immense but hidden flow of interaction, a dynamic process of action and consequence that doesn't stop with us and our particular role.

We don't know the ultimate unfolding of any story; certainly not enough to decide that what we do has no effect. When we stand before a chasm of futility, it is, first of all, faith in this larger perspective that enables us to go on.

Dealing with Deadlines

"I don't need time, I need a deadline."
— Duke Ellington

Dan Ariely is a Duke University professor who conducted an interesting experiment about ten years ago. He set up three classes, and each class had three weeks to finish three papers. Class A had to turn in all three papers on the last day of class; Class B had to pick three different deadlines and stick to them; and Class C had to turn in one paper a week. If the papers were late, there were severe penalties to the final grade. Which class had the best grades? Class C, the one with three specific deadlines, did the best. Class B, which had to pick deadlines ahead of time but had complete freedom, did the second best, and the group whose only deadline was the last day, Class A, did the worst.

What can we learn from this experiment about procrastination? The students who could pick any three deadlines (B) tended to spread them out. They expected that they would procrastinate, so they naturally set up different deadlines. That way, they wouldn't be working on all three papers at the last minute. The students who had no choice at all about the deadlines (Group C - the deadlines were spread out for them) actually did slightly better. The students with no guidelines at all (A) tended to put off their work until the last week for all three papers. They did the worst.

So if you know that you procrastinate on particular kinds of tasks, you are actually better off, because you have the ability to set up an approach that factors in your tendency to procrastinate. But the real difference between coping with procrastination and overcoming it is … feelings! Most procrastination is caused by a tendency to make a decision, in the present moment, based on what we feel like doing at that moment. And if we don't feel like doing something NOW, then we're not likely to feel like doing it later, because (are you following this?) later will just be another NOW. If you don't feel like doing your taxes NOW, just accept that you'll probably never feel like doing them.

The fundamental change we need is a shift from a feeling-centered approach to decisions to a purpose-centered approach. The question isn't "What do I feel like doing?" but, rather, "what needs to be done?" All the time management systems in the world won't really help us very much until we've developed the capacity to make decisions based on purpose rather than feelings. And this is one of the reasons that Morita therapy is so valuable. It teaches us how to do that. We learn that we can coexist with our feelings and take them along for the ride. We don't fight them. We don't fix them. We don't transform them. We coexist with them, while we move forward and take appropriate action.

It takes maturity to work on something far in advance of a deadline if the activity isn't something we like. Most of us need the pressure of a deadline closing in to kick us into action. Why? Because the feeling of discomfort or aversion we associate with the work is stronger than the feeling of anxiety we have about getting it done. So we wait until the feeling of fear or anxiety becomes stronger than the aversion to the activity. It's a battle of feelings. The alternative is to simply do the work because it's what needs to be done, regardless of how we feel. We can call this maturity, or self-discipline, but it's really about developing the skill to coexist with our feelings and take action anyway.

Finishing: Big Girls Don't Tri (Or Do They?)

MARGARET MCKENZIE & JENNIFER BUCKO LAMPLOUGH

*M*y daughter-in-law refers to herself as a "big girl." I call her a strong, determined woman. In the seven years I've known her, since my son first introduced her to our family, she has written and published two books, completed an MBA, and facilitated an "idea incubator" at the college where she is the Dean of Integrative Studies.

When Jen decided to do a triathlon this summer, nine years after her first effort, I had no doubt that she would finish. However, she had concerns. She was much heavier than she was when she did the first one. She was heavier than any of the other participants. During the time she was training, she kept a blog titled **Big Girls Don't Tri... or do they?** She was accompanied, in training and in the race, by two lifelong friends, Meg and Liz. I was there when she crossed the finish line on June 11, 2011. It was an inspiring moment. The blog entry she wrote afterwards reminded me of Morita therapy principles, and how much her efforts embodied these ideas.

Her triathlon included three legs: swimming, biking and running. She started off strong, finishing the swim in less time than she expected. During the 14-mile bike ride, she fell behind, and eventually was in last place, the police *escort tailing her down the road. She finished biking, and then came the run. This is how she described her experience…*

Here came the hardest part. As I started out on the 4.1 mile run, all of these people were done with the race and were coming back to get their bikes. They were done and I was just starting the hardest part, and my mind went haywire. My inner monologue sounded something like this:

"People are done. DONE. Oh my God. I can't do this. I have my phone. I can call Mike. He'll come get me. All of these people are done? Oh my God, I'm last. Everyone is staring at me. I can't do this, I can't do this, I can't do this."

I couldn't stop the horrible thoughts. My legs felt like lead. Was I moving forward or just standing there? I couldn't tell. I kept walking. I wasn't about to try and run yet. What's running? Am I moving? People were cheering me on, yelling, "You can do it." I wanted to flip them off, or throw a hammer at their heads, but they were just being nice so I smiled and said "Thanks."

One foot in front of the other. That's what I kept saying to myself. *One foot in front of the other.* Then I saw them — my husband, my father-in-law, my mother-in-law and my good friend Meg, who'd just finished her race with a personal record. Sh*t. Here come the tears. "I'm struggling!" I shouted as I passed their sweet, cheering faces. Meg asked if I wanted her to come with me. "No," I squeaked out and kept walking. And crying. Then I heard her run up to me. "I'm coming with you," she said. Okay. She just finished this race, and started the last three miles of it all over again with me. Thank God she did. She saved me. She got me to stop crying and hyperventilating. My shorts were driving me crazy, so she carried them for me. She got an extra cup of water for me at each water stop, and carried it for me. She saved me. We walked the whole thing, and came around a corner that was about 150 yards from the finish line, when I saw Liz, the third member of our triathlon trio, waiting for us. She finished strong and came back to find us. She was flying high, and her happiness and endorphin buzz filled me with energy. One hundred yards left. "Run it in!" Meg yelled, and gave me a push.

I started running, and then all I could see was a sea of people yelling and clapping for me. Me. They were rhythmically chanting my name – *Jen-ny, Jen-ny.* And then, there it was: *The Finish Line.* The beautiful, glorious finish line. So I ran and sobbed and ran and sobbed and crossed the finish line, falling into the arms of my dear, sweet husband, my two best friends who came out to see us race, and my mother-in-law and father-in-law, and we all laughed and cried and cheered. All of these strangers were slapping me on the back, hugging me, congratulating me, bringing me water and Gatorade. Telling me I was an inspiration. It was one of the most touching, exciting, slightly humiliating, overwhelming and fulfilling moments of my life. I finished.

I finished strong. Liz told me she saw people quitting after the bike. But I didn't quit. I finished. Last, but certainly not least.

Afterword: *It turned out that crossing the finish line was not the end but the beginning for Jen. In the three years since this article appeared in* Thirty Thousand Days, *she has repeated the Batavia Tri, completed a half marathon, done an "Ironwoman" Triathlon and run countless 5K and 10K races.*

Obsessed with the Unfinished

Michael C. Gilbert wrote a thought-provoking essay about our preoccupation with the unfinished. He says,

If you were to judge your tasks by how much attention and emotional investment they get, you would think that only those things that are not yet done are of any importance. Do you understand what I'm saying? We don't build up a list of completed tasks over the course of the day, we cross off a list of things to do. We don't put up a sticky note as a reminder of an important accomplishment, we put up notes of things that we need to do.

There is something horribly out of balance in this. Through force of repetition, this habit deludes us into seeing the deficits and scarcities in our lives more easily than the accomplishments and resources. It distorts and undermines our motivation because the future never really comes and we don't adequately internalize our completed work. I truly believe that the message we get, deep inside, is that only the unfinished is important.

Now, you probably have used some type of to-do list, whether on a sheet of scrap paper or on your computer. And you know the experience Gilbert is talking about. We start off with our inventory of things undone and then race against time to check them off. That list keeps reminding us of what awaits us. Our energy is drained from attention to the present, or reflection on the past, to what we need to do next. This is how we create the rushed and chaotic pace of our life.

Let me contrast this with learning to play music. My children have studied either violin or piano for seven years using a method from Japan called Suzuki Music Education. When you begin studying piano you receive a book, which has about twenty songs in it. You start by learning to play *Mary Had a Little Lamb*. You may glance at the remaining pages in the book, but virtually all your energy goes into that one song. And when you master *Mary Had a Little Lamb* (can one ever master such a classic?) you move on to the next song. But you continue to play *Mary Had a Little Lamb* as a review song. All those hours working on a piece of music provide a harvest of joy as you continue to play. And when you've learned all twenty songs in Book I, there is a recital, which is a celebration of all the music you have learned and can share with others. There is sanity in this process that allows us to concentrate fully on the work before us, and then celebrate its completion before a community of friends and family.

Ideally we need a process of doing our daily work in which we can immerse ourselves completely in our current task without the distraction of the unfinished. When you go to the doctor, you may only get 15 minutes, but if that 15 minutes is truly devoted to your medical needs, you feel attended to. Contrast this with the doctor who juggles several patients at once or sends signals of impatience that make it clear he has mountains of other patients waiting. You sense that they can't wait for you to leave so the doctor can get on with treating the next person. And the next person gets the same treatment.

When we finish a task we should take a moment to reflect. How were we supported? What did we learn? What problems did we cause others? I find that when I reflect on a completed issue of *Thirty Thousand Days* or the treehouse I built, I am reminded that what has been done would be impossible without the help of other people and objects. Rather than a sense of pride, I feel a sense of gratitude to all those who were part of the effort. Rather than feel overwhelmed with all that has to be done I feel connected with everything in the universe that makes it possible just to buy groceries at the supermarket.

A to-do list can be a valuable tool. Writing down what needs doing can free your mind from having to remember. But a successful day is not determined by what we've left undone. It has to do with integrity, kindness and a sense of gratitude for what I have received. It has to do with the quality of my attention and the way I treated others. It has to do with presence and purpose. Let's not measure the value of our lives by the actions we didn't take.

Impermanence and Legos

"Impermanence is the essence of everything."
- Pema Chodron

Nothings stays the same. We don't have to study Asian philosophy or Buddhism to know that. It's obvious if we just look around – at the seasons, our kids, our cars, even our bodies. But knowing that everything in life is impermanent doesn't prevent us from resisting change and complaining about it. We don't like it when the brakes on our car wear out. Or when our skin gets wrinkled. Or when our kids go off to college or one of our parents die. We work so hard to get things where we want them. And once we accomplish that formidable task, we want them to stay that way so we can relax and enjoy life.

I recently watched the *Lego Movie*. It's not the kind of film I would normally watch, but I read some interesting comments about it, so my daughter and I spent several hours on the sofa, watching these animated little Lego figures have an adventure. The villain in the film is a character named Lord Business. Lord Business doesn't like change. He doesn't like it when people tear down and rebuild things (*isn't that what you do with Legos?*). He comes up with a solution – glue everything together. That's his answer to impermanence – defeat it! Stop it.

The protagonists in the film are a collection of Lego superheroes who are *Master Builders*. They are creative and energetic. They love making new things, which requires taking parts from old things. They are forces for change. They are Lego manifestations of impermanence. So the stage for the metaphorical battle is now set – stability vs impermanence.

When I was a child, I didn't have Legos – I had model airplanes which I put together with glue. Once you built the plane it was done. You put it on the shelf and bought another kit. But my youngest daughter spent years playing with an exceptionally large collection of Legos. She would spend days building an amazing spaceship. Then she would show it to us and play with it for a while. Eventually, it was taken apart for the next project. Legos have past lives. One day they're part of a space ship. The next day they're part of a castle.

It reminds me of the Tibetan monks who spend a week or more creating a beautifully designed mandala made of sand. And then when they finish it, and everyone has admired the craftsmanship, they destroy it. From sand to mandala and back to sand. Impermanence.

One of the challenges of living in an impermanent world is that change often requires action on our part. Winter turns to spring and we have to get the garden ready for planting. The lawnmower breaks and we have to repair it. Our hair falls out in the bathtub and we have to clean it. And then there are the larger challenges like job layoffs, divorce, death, bankruptcy. Each change presents us with a new "what do I need to do now?" riddle. It's tiring. It's stressful. All this change. All this responding to change. Exhausting.

No wonder we begin to distrust change. No wonder we feel anxious when we know a change is on the horizon. There is a *Lord Business* in each of us that just wants to get things in place and then glue them together. Of course, we can't. But it's tempting to try.

Whether we like it or not, we have to work with impermanence. And the way we work with it is to respond to change according to what needs to be done. It's not about how we feel (i.e. frustrated) or what we're thinking (doom and gloom thoughts). It's about taking action according to the needs of the situation. We accept the circumstances that we cannot change. We accept the internal reaction we're having – our feelings and thoughts – that we also cannot change. And we try to simply step back and look clearly: What are the needs of the situation? That's how we know what to do and when to do it.

It's not easy: responding to the impermanence of our lives when we're faced with disappointment, distress, or disaster. And it's not easy taking action when, inside, we're fired up with anxiety, fear and anger. But there's a saving grace in the situation. You know what it is?

Impermanence.

The situation you're faced with will change, evolve, unfold. It always does. The feelings you're feeling will dissolve, disappear and be replaced by other feelings. They always have. You don't have to deal with this forever. You don't have to feel this way forever.

If you don't like what's happening, rest assured, it will change.

If you are pleased with the situation, rest assured, it will change.

Those are the rules. Enjoy the game. Build something. Tear it down. Have fun. It will be over all too soon.

Compassionate Action

*Real action is meant to comfort others, meant to
demonstrate love and concern. If somebody falls
down and you just look and smile at him, then
you're obviously not interested in helping him.
If you actually go forward, pick him up and you
can find out whether he's hurt himself, help him
to clean his wound. If he's bruised,
then you clean up his bruises, you put a little
bit of plaster on it — that shows that you're
really concerned.
But if you just stand there, smile and say, "Oh
how are you, are you feeling bad?" and you
don't make a move to do anything about that,
then nobody is going to believe that you're
really concerned even if you do speak the same
language. Actions do speak louder than words.*

– AUNG SAN SUU KYI

Just Do It

MARGARET MCKENZIE

Korean Zen Master Seung Sahn knew no English when he came to the United States. He only had a strong desire to teach American students. He found a place to live in Providence, Rhode Island and took a job repairing washing machines. Quickly, some young American students showed up at his door. At first he used an interpreter to teach them, but soon he began learning English. As he taught Zen to his young students, he would often learn just one sentence of English that encapsulated the Zen principle he wanted to teach, and for the next few weeks his students would hear only that one sentence.

"Only go straight, don't know" was one.

"Try, try, try for ten thousand years" was another.

And a third, a decade before Nike used it to sell shoes, was the phrase "just do it."

The phrase had two slightly different meanings. First, it was to do only one thing at a time and to do it wholeheartedly. "When you are eating, only eat; when you are sleeping, only sleep." No multitasking allowed!

The second meaning seems a little more elusive. "Go for it, don't hold back. Don't let the 'small I' of your ego stop you from doing what needs to be done, from taking the risk." I don't think he meant "Just do whatever comes to your mind." I think he was referring to instances where we see a clear direction for ourselves, but then hesitate and let our second thoughts hold us back.

He categorized three habits of mind that stop us from "just doing it."

• *Checking:* defined as second-guessing ourselves or others;

• *Holding:* hanging on to feelings about an interaction after it was completed; for example, bearing a grudge; and

• *Making:* taking the words or actions of another and inventing a story about what our mind thinks those actions/words meant. (*I call this finding a thread and knitting a sweater out of it.*)

It's checking that often gets in the way of the spirit of "just do it." We have an idea—to give something, to teach something, to push our boundaries—then we hear the checking voice in the background.

"No, that's too hard."

"I don't have enough experience."

"I don't have time right now."

"I might look foolish."

"I might fail."

Actually, some of those voices came up for me as I thought about writing this essay. When we "just do it" we may put ourselves on the line, opening ourselves to both praise and blame. The psychiatrist Shoma Morita gave us a great antidote for the checking voice:

Be clear about your purpose, accept your feelings and thoughts, and then just do what needs doing.

Vipassana teacher Joseph Goldstein talks about this when he speaks of his practice of generosity. He says that when he has an idea to give something, he always follows through. *"Thoughts will arise — maybe I won't do this, maybe I need this, maybe I'll hold back -- but the practice is I always do it."*

Similarly, Pema Chodron relates a story of giving a sweater to a young woman. Chodron loved the sweater, which was cashmere and a maroon color that matched her nun's robes. All the way to the train station, she had a war in her mind about giving it away, but when they reached the station, she graciously parted with the sweater.

Often, we think of the teachings of Morita therapy in connection with our neurotic feelings of fear and anxiety, but a more subtle application of these principles is related to feelings that arise when our best selves — our generous, kind, and caring selves — want to step forward. It is easy to listen to the voices in our heads that say, "No, hang on to that... I might need it... I don't have time."

We can listen to the voices and then consider our purpose — to be fully human in our connections with others and... *just do it.*

Don't Expect Applause

What this slogan means is don't expect thanks. . . More than expect thanks, it would be helpful just to expect the unexpected; then you might be curious and inquisitive about what comes in the door. We can begin to open our hearts to others when we have no hope of getting anything back. We just do it for its own sake. We can thank others, but we should give up all hope of getting thanked in return. Simply keep the door open without expectations.

- Pema Chodron

Taking Action in Relationships

SUSAN PAGE

A cting "as if" simply means choosing "nice" behavior, even when you don't feel like it. It means not allowing your feelings to dictate how you will behave, but instead, motivated by your desire to become a more spiritual person, choosing how you will behave. When you act as if, you are no longer at the mercy of your feelings or your mood. Here are five tips:

1.Start small. You can act as if you are a loving, adoring spouse, even if you don't feel that way, for just five minutes, for a half hour, or for one evening a week.

The next time something upsets or angers you, think about acting as if. Try it for just one minute.

Recently, as I returned to my car because I knew my parking meter would be running out, I saw a meter maid writing out a ticket.

"Wait! I'm here. The meter just ran out!" I cried out.

But she wouldn't tear up the ticket. I don't do well when I have no control over what I consider to be a dumb situation. I felt my face flush, my heart start to race. But because I'm writing about spiritual behavior every day right now, the thought "act spiritually" went through my head. I took a deep breath. And then I smiled. Not a sarcastic smile. It was an act-as-if smile. I couldn't bring myself to say anything nice to the meter maid, but at least I didn't say anything nasty to her. I kept smiling. By the time I was driving away, I was thinking, *So a parking ticket, so big deal.*

2. You can also act as if, not in response to a situation, but as a proactive way of taking initiative or providing leadership.

What do you want from your partner? Do you wish he or she were more demonstrative? Do you wish you had fun more often? Would you like more romance?

Create these activities yourself. Ask yourself, "How would I behave if I were a totally loving spouse?" You might do favors for your partner. You might greet him or her enthusiastically when you come together at the end of the workday.

What do you wish you could do with your partner? Don't wait.

As one workshop participant told us after two weeks of experimenting with acting as if, "It's so easy to get affection; just give it."

3. Don't be discouraged if your feelings or your mate's responses don't change quickly and dramatically. Patiently proceed with acting like a loving spouse on a regular basis, even if it is just for a few minutes at a time, even if you see no direct results or changes.

Remember, in the midst of a difficult incident or a time when you feel very bad, you cannot change your feelings. They are simply there. You feel angry. You feel afraid. You can't make your feeling go away by an act of will. Nor can you change the other person who is part of this situation, as we have already discussed. But you do have control over your own behavior. You can make a deliberate choice to act as if you feel good. And when you do, you open up a whole range of new possibilities.

4. Be prepared for voices of resistance within you.

My partner doesn't deserve this loving behavior. This is too one-sided. I shouldn't have to be nice. This is too fake. I can't pretend I feel loving. I don't!

It's okay for these voices to be there. Just don't let them win.

As Dan Millman observes in *The Way of the Peaceful Warrior*, "Old urges will continue to arise, perhaps for years. Urges do not matter, actions do."

5. Actions matter. When you are trying to create a happy, safe atmosphere in your marriage, actions are what will make this happen.

Apathy won't help you. Talking won't make any difference. Blaming will keep you stuck for years. Only new behavior, even when you don't feel like doing it, will make changes start to happen. As we've said, you will never feel your way to a new way of acting, but you can absolutely act your way to a new way of feeling.

Defeating the Demons of Inaction

Fear

One of the most common obstacles to taking action is fear. Strong feelings bubble up inside us. Our body tenses up. We begin to imagine the road up ahead – failure, embarrassment, rejection, pain, even death. In the face of fear we may find ourselves "frozen" in an iceberg of inaction. Or we may find ourselves running away, rather than facing the thing which we fear.

Fear is not necessarily our enemy, though it usually feels that way. Fear can make us think twice about risky behavior, it can warn us to tread cautiously, and it can remind us that there are consequences we'd rather avoid. That surge of fear may be prompting us in a healthy direction, in spite of the fact that it is disruptive to our sense of inner harmony.

"If we did not have fear, I do not know how many more people would die in traffic accidents every day. When a car is rushing toward you, you will be run over if you are perfectly calm and collected."
— Takehisa Kora, M.D.

Many years ago I was running a monthly Morita group in New York City. I was riding on the subway at about 10pm from the Upper East Side to the Staten Island Ferry. I did not live in New York, and I was wary of the city, even during the day. As I was sitting in the subway car, I drifted into thoughts about the day and mentally replayed a tape of some of my experiences. Then I felt a noticeable bump in the ride and, being startled, I looked up. There was nothing there. Actually, there was nobody there. I was the only person in the subway car.

Almost instantly, I felt a surge of fear. A flood of adrenaline rushed through my chest and shoulders. My breathing got faster. My body felt hot. I looked around again. I got up. I walked to the end of the subway car and through the door into the next car, where there were 8-10 people sitting quietly. One of the things I realized that night was that fear can be energy. Up until the point when I felt afraid, I was rather tired, and my mind was unfocused and drifting. But when I sat down in the next car, just a few minutes later, I was wide awake and full of energy. I was attentive to my surroundings. I felt as if I could play basketball.

So fear can be our friend, and it can provide energy for action. But in many cases, fear prevents us from taking action when action is called for. It can surface when we are not in imminent danger. Fear can run wild when we are doing exactly what we need to be doing -- when we really care about what we're doing and deeply wish to succeed. How do we stay on course when fear is flashing and burning within? What is the best strategy for coping skillfully with fear?

We must learn the skill of coexisting with fear.

The Buddhist teacher Chogyam Trungpa used the term "fearlessness." He said that fearlessness is not freedom from fear or having less fear. It is "going beyond" fear.

The best strategy for coping skillfully with fear is to develop the ability to coexist ... to accept our internal state, whether we like it or not, and continue on with our plans, knowing that our feelings will change soon enough.

What does it mean to coexist with fear? It means that we are willing to be with our state of fear without trying to change it or run away from it.

Feelings are sensations. The ability to tolerate sensations we'd rather not have is supremely important. Without such tolerance, our lives remain needlessly vulnerable to our wild and fickle feelings, and our plans get needlessly derailed. Without such tolerance we can become preoccupied to an unhealthy degree with our private internal experience, and thereby become distracted from the world around us, the needs of others, and the tasks at hand. It is difficult to build our dreams without coexisting with the feelings that come up in the process of creating those dreams.

Notice the feeling, recognize it for what it is, take a deep breath, and shift your energies to that which needs doing.

"Right now, I am feeling a great deal of fear."

We notice fear. We acknowledge it. We accept it. But we don't put fear in charge. We don't let it decide what we do and don't do. And at some point, we may learn to harness the energy of fear and use it to take action in response to the situation we are facing.

"When I left my job after 13 years, I initially felt as if I had lost my right arm. I had no other experience in my work life because I had worked there since graduating from college. After I grieved my losses (loss of seeing friends every day, the loss of a routine, the loss of steady income, etc.) I became very scared. However, I read somewhere a saying that helped me feel the fear and do it anyway!
This saying became my motto.
When I was scared to make a networking call to someone I didn't know, I would be petrified, read that saying and make the call. The point is that fear actually helped me. It energized me. My situation changed when I put the energy to good use instead of becoming anxious and fearful."

— Carol Jennett

Indecision

How do we continue to get things done when we don't know what things need doing, when we are unclear about the next step to take? Most of us have had the experience of being stuck in an indecisive mode, not moving forward or backward or even to the side, just hovering in flight, waiting or searching for a sign that will indicate the best direction.

It can be difficult to move forward without clarity, for clarity of purpose often brings with it enthusiasm and energy. But when clarity is lacking, what is the best response? If clarity is still elusive after giving the issue some thoughtful consideration and doing some good homework, what are our options? Afraid to make the wrong choice, we can wait and hope for a decision to become obvious. We try to think through the issue in our minds. We analyze it and ruminate about it.

But we can't figure out life in our minds. Life is resolved through life itself.

Even when we think we've figured everything out intellectually, life seldom plays out as a perfect replica of our mental plan.

So when we are confronted by indecision, we need to take action despite our doubts or confusion. We need to move forward, even if we're only taking small steps. Those steps, regardless of which direction they go in, are likely to give us new information and experience. Our actions send ripples into the world.

The situation may change or reveal itself in a new way once we have moved to a new vantage point.

Think of your life as a movie you are watching. You are midway through the movie and you don't know what is going to happen. *But you're not supposed to know what is going to happen.* The movie is not over yet. This is the challenge posed by the demon of indecision: Can you move forward in the face of uncertainty? Can you co-exist with confusion and not-knowing and take the next step?

Small steps are an elegant approach to indecision. That's because each of those small steps sends ripples out into the world. Your situation is never the same from day to day, because the world is in a dynamic state of flux. Once you take a small step you get new information and now you can consider the situation from a different perspective.

Ultimately, you may need to make a decision, even though you lack clarity and confidence. You'll feel confused. You'll feel anxious. You'll wonder whether or not you're making the "right" decision.

And somewhere along the road you may discover that there is no such thing as the "right" decision. There is just the action you take and the new situation you face as a result. And that discovery becomes an important tool for taming the demon of indecision. *There's no right decision.* It's better to put your energy into doing the best with whatever situation arises, than getting lost in the anxiety of trying to make the "right" choice.

Discouragement

*A student asked Soen Nakagawa
during a meditation retreat,*

"I am very discouraged. What should I do?"

Soen replied, "Encourage others."

One of my favorite stories is J.R.R. Tolkien's trilogy *The Lord of the Rings.* Almost from the beginning, the quest of the fellowship is hopeless. The odds against them seem insurmountable. The enemy is strong, vast and cunning. The fellowship, on the other hand, struggles with contentiousness and betrayal within its own ranks. Ultimately, several members of the fellowship are killed, and the rest are divided and even captured. The story is a treatise on coping with discouragement.

Most of us face discouragement from time to time. Either we are confused, overwhelmed, or simply feel we lack what it takes to cope successfully with the situation at hand. So now what do we do? We might simply succumb to the despair of the situation and allow it to immobilize us. Or we may look to others – teachers, family members, friends, books, affirmations – to guide us out of our discouragement. But the Zen teacher

Soen Nakagawa offers us a brilliant solution: Encourage Others!

Well, how can we encourage others when we're discouraged ourselves? Normally we think that there is a person who is discouraged and that is the person who is suffering. And there is a person who encourages them, and that is the person who is doing well – who is wise and has his act together. But Nakagawa Roshi says that when we are suffering, that is when we should provide encouragement to others. He doesn't say, "first get yourself together, and then give others encouragement." It's the act of encouraging others that heals our own discouragement.

The secret underlying this process has to do with attention. When we are discouraged, all of our attention is on ourselves. "My life is so hard. I don't have the strength. I'm disappointed and demoralized. I'm overwhelmed."

Our attention is glued to our own suffering. If you think of your attention as a kind of fertilizer, you realize that by focusing your attention on your own suffering you are actually helping it to grow and deepen its roots in your mind and body. But to encourage others, you have to shift your attention to the suffering of the other person. "How is their life hard? What is the nature of their difficulty? How can I support them?" When you shift your attention to encouraging someone else, you have removed the nourishment for your own suffering.

Where is your suffering when you're not paying attention to it?

St Francis said, "Grant that I may not so much seek to be consoled, as to console." The entire prayer is about shifting one's attention away from oneself. The fact that it's a prayer is testimony to its difficulty. So we can make this our practice and sometimes we'll do it well and at other times we'll just fall on our face. If you fall on your face often enough, you get discouraged. And then . . .

Perfectionism

"Give up on yourself. Begin taking action now,
while being neurotic or imperfect, or a
procrastinator or unhealthy or lazy or any other
label by which you inaccurately describe
yourself. Go ahead and be the best imperfect
person you can be and get started on those
things you want to accomplish before you die. "
— Shoma Morita, M.D.

Perfectionism may prevent us from starting something. Or, as we stay focused on the imperfections of what we're doing, it may keep us from finishing something. We'd like to write the perfect book, the perfect poem, create the perfect sculpture, or even plant a perfect garden. The realization that we may fail can result in a failure to even attempt what we wish to do.

Of course, it's not that we think that what we're doing needs to be perfect. We just don't want to make a mistake. Yet as human beings, we're likely to make mistakes. If we think our talent is so great that we shouldn't make a mistake, then we have a very grandiose attitude about ourselves. If you think about it, there is a relationship between perfectionism and grandiosity. If you think that what you do should be perfect, than you must have a very high opinion of yourself. On the other hand, if you assess your abilities realistically, you are likely to discover some humility and accept a more realistic perspective about what you are doing.

A common problem caused by perfectionism is not finishing something, or being very late. We're not willing to say "it's finished" and send our work out into the world because we continue to see the possibilities for improvement. In some cases, this creates significant problems for others who are expecting our work at a given time.

So what is the best way to overcome perfectionism? First, we have to understand that mistakes are unavoidable. In many cases, the mistake is less important than what you do after you've made a mistake. You may get discouraged, demoralized or angry at yourself. But once a mistake is made, we must simply respond to the new reality. What action do I need to take now? According to psychiatrist Rudolf Dreikurs, *"What is needed is not concern with what we've done wrong, but the determination to meet the demands of the moment."*

So perhaps the best way to confront the demon of perfectionism is to accept him as an ideal, but to be realistic about what you can do and accept the likelihood that you will make mistakes or fail.

Television

You may be surprised to see television here as one of the "demons." Unlike the other demons, it has a body, a physical form. It sits there in the living room or bedroom and looks rather innocent (when it's turned off). Yet the passivity that TV engenders makes it a truly dangerous piece of equipment. Of course there is the commercialism that TV is built upon, which keeps our minds (and those of our kids) endlessly stoked toward desires for more stuff. There's also the poor quality of much of the programming itself, which dulls the mind and flattens the spirit. But above and beyond all of that, there is the passivity that TV brings about, which results in wasted time, lost dreams, untapped potential, secondhand living, overweight bodies, unchallenged minds, lost opportunities and missed connections with family, friends, nature, and life.

Many of us eased into the TV habit very easily and naturally as youngsters, growing up in households where the TV flicker was a given. Today, the television is distracting American families for six to eight hours per day in many homes. The sounds of TV vary wildly, for sure, but many people develop a strong attachment to the lively or cheerful banter that fills an otherwise quiet or tense space. We may become very fond of TV characters — charming, beautiful, witty and comfortably familiar. We enjoy witnessing their misadventures, with our feet up and our own lives temporarily on hold.

Les MacFarlane, a teacher in Ottawa, described one of the experiences that helped him "kick the habit" many years ago:

"An exercise that was really helpful was writing my own eulogy. Nowhere in the life that I had created for myself through my eulogy did it say 'Les MacFarlane was a television aficionado who saw every episode of Seinfeld...*twice.' What I became aware of were the things I wanted to do: be a responsible father and husband, practice Zen more intensely, and become a writer. For the first time I saw that television was getting in the way of attaining those goals."*

We can easily watch television for several hours a day "to relax" and then minimize the effect it's having on getting important things done in our lives One of my students calculated the amount of time she had spent watching TV during the past five years. Her total was 4,000 hours. That's the equivalent of going to work each day for 500 straight days and doing nothing but watching television! She was then asked to make a list of the meaningful activities that could have filled that amount of time. Without TV, her life would have been dramatically different during those five years.

Besides the time television steals from our lives, the more subtle strategy of this demon is to shorten our attention span, which serves to strengthen another demon - boredom. Dr. Mathew Dumont writes, in *The American Journal of Psychiatry,* that *"apart from the rapid and violent content of the programs, there are incessant changes of camera and focus, so that the viewer's reference point shifts every few seconds. This technique literally programs a short attention span."*

If TV is playing too big a role in your life – if it keeps you up too late, if it keeps you in a trance too often, try one of these options:

♦   Put your TV in the closet for a month. Take it out no more than once a week to watch a particular show, if you like, and then put it back.

♦   Get rid of it altogether.

The alternative to TV is to fill your time with real life. By next year, you'll have accomplished a lot more, and you'll free up additional wall/floor space.

Boredom

"Monotony is the law of nature. Look at the monotonous manner in which the sun rises."
— *Mahatma Gandhi*

When I'm involved in an exciting activity such as white-water rafting, I generally have little difficulty keeping my attention focused on what I'm doing. During those moments in which I am maneuvering through frisky waters, my mind is not likely to wander too far off course. Without much deliberate effort on my part, my attention is riveted to the waves as they hit and to the raft as it responds. Little else is likely to compete for my attention during these thrilling moments. Financial worries, anxiety about my health, and interpersonal concerns are unlikely to arise while my attention is highly focused. The exhilaration and novelty of such an experience is almost impossible to compete with.

I am also very likely to do what needs to be done in those moments, at least to the best of my ability. The partnership between single-minded focus and clarity of purpose is a powerful one, which translates easily and naturally into action steps. Add to that mix the consequence that is likely to result with sincere and diligent effort on my part, and we have the ideal ingredients needed for getting a job done -- for doing what we are called upon to do.

Even when the environment is tamer than a white-water river, if it is new and novel it will be relatively easy to pay attention to. One of the reasons traveling is so satisfying may have to do with the fact that we get a break from our typical self-preoccupations, at least to some degree. Surrounded by the unfamiliar, our senses tend to perk up. Noticing the details of architecture and foliage in New Orleans is easier for those with a Yankee background.

But of course the reverse is also true. On our own familiar hometown streets, our minds often start wandering in an effort to discover more interesting and entertaining subjects. To pay attention to the familiar often takes a more deliberate effort. Our minds, particularly if accustomed to a high level of distraction and stimulation over time, often find it hard to settle down. Staying focused on a task may quickly be experienced as monotonous or boring, and our energy for the task will drag.

The Demon of Boredom usually employs distraction as his tool. He lures our minds into connecting with something other than what we need to do. If there is nothing in the outside world to capture our attention, the Demon of Boredom will seduce us through our internal world of daydreams, thoughts and ideas. Though he works on our minds, his ultimate goal is to change the effort of our bodies. It is the boundary between mind and body where he can be defeated.

For as many times as he distracts us we can simply counter by returning our attention to what it is we need to do. Ultimately if we maintain self-control over our behavior, this demon can be defeated. If we remain seated at our desk, writing a report, or standing by the sink, washing the dishes, we can persist alongside our boredom and finish what we need to do. As with fear, our main strategy is to coexist with the thoughts and feelings of being bored, while continuing to work on our task.

Clarity of purpose is a critical factor when dealing with boredom. Tolerating the experience of boredom is much more manageable once the reason for doing so is clear. If I am midway through my work on a tedious project, which long ago consumed what little interest I may have begun with, my greatest salvation comes from understanding why that project is worth doing.

Boredom may be an indicator that we are not paying attention to the details of what we are doing. When we pay attention to details, our curiosity is often awakened. At the ToDo Institute we have a collection of small portable microscopes. We take them on hikes in the woods. You can stand in one spot and spend forty-five minutes studying objects under the microscope – objects that would generally get little attention. The face of a spider. The bark of a hickory tree. A blade of grass or even the weave of the cloth on your own pair of blue jeans. Curiosity is a path that leads to details. And details are the antidote to boredom.

"If I insist that my work be rewarding, that it mustn't be tedious or monotonous, I'm in trouble. . . Time after time it fails to become so. So I get more agitated about it, I fight with people about it, I make more demands about it . . . It's ridiculous to demand that work always be pleasurable, because work is not necessarily pleasing; sometimes it is, sometimes it isn't . If we're detached and simply pick up the job we have to do and go ahead and do it, it's usually fairly satisfying. Even jobs that are repugnant or dull or tedious tend to be quite satisfying, once we get right down to doing them. . . One of the routine jobs I get every once in a while comes from putting out a little magazine. You have to sort the pages. It's a simple, routine, mechanical sort of job. . . I never realized that this would be one of the most satisfying parts of the whole thing, just standing there and sorting pages. This happens when we just do what we have to do."

– THOMAS MERTON

Difficulty

*"Sometimes we try to escape from something
we have to do, we dislike to do, because we think
it's too difficult. But we don't know what we
"can" or "cannot" do until we challenge it
directly."*
— Hiroaki Masuda

When we say something is "too hard" to do, what does that really mean? Unless we've already sincerely tackled the task and given it our best, it means that we are not up to the challenge. But thoughts are not reality. They are not necessarily trustworthy.

Frequently our minds create boundaries about what we can and cannot accomplish, but often these boundaries fall far short of what we can really accomplish when we make our best effort. In essence, *our minds often underestimate what our bodies can do.*

The Demon of Difficulty tries to persuade us to always remain in our "comfort zone." When we do things we already know how to do, we usually can remain safely in our comfort zone. During our residential training programs at the ToDo Institute, we ask that people not use any animal products in the meals they prepare. To accommodate this guideline, people can easily resort to a dinner of pasta with marinara sauce and salad. So we encourage people to go beyond their comfort zone and try something new, something they haven't cooked before. What about making Chinese cuisine or some Thai food? Initially people may think, "Oh my goodness! I can't make Thai food. Are you crazy? But that thought is simply the Demon of Difficulty urging us to stay within our comfort zone.

To overcome this demon, we need to take the risks of doing things that stimulate feelings of discomfort, fear, anxiety, and confusion. We need to develop the capacity to coexist with these feelings as we tackle a new or challenging task. We need to accept the possibility that we might fail or make mistakes and move forward cautiously, but, nevertheless, move forward.

The Demon of Difficulty is easily overcome by repeated success. He first appeared to us as children when we were attempting to walk. But our curiosity and "beginner's minds" weren't about to let him restrict us to crawling the rest of our life. Can we find that curiosity and beginner's mind again as we consider learning how to play the piano or fix the gears on our bicycle?

In some cases, our assessment of the difficulty of a task is based primarily on its complexity. We look at the overall task — writing a book, for example — and conclude that it's simply overwhelming and beyond our reach. But a book comes into being through a long series of small tasks and decisions, each one done individually, in its own moment. If you can write one page, you can write one chapter. If you can write one chapter, perhaps three. If you can write three chapters, you can write a book.

The Demon of Difficulty is relentless. You can defeat him in one battle, but he just returns later and chooses a different venue. Don't bother with self-talk, trying to convince yourself you have confidence, or with artificial efforts to pump up your self-esteem. He already has well-designed counterpunches for those moves. Simply move forward and take action. Be persistent. In some cases, the outcome you achieve will be different from what you were hoping for. But regardless of the outcome, you can keep this demon in his place by giving your all to a project, demonstrating that you are not intimidated by doubts and fears about difficulty. The way to overcome this demon is by showing him he was wrong.

One More Thing:

Don't Just Be in the Audience

Think about how often you are part of an audience. You read books that other people wrote. You watch movies that other people filmed. You watch your kids or grandkids play soccer. You watch sports or sitcoms. You read poems by Mary Oliver. Or listen to an audio book on mindfulness.

Everything you're reading, watching and listening to involved a creative process. A process that probably involved more than one person. You get to witness the outcome. You get to be in the audience.

There's nothing wrong with being in the audience. You can applaud. You can cheer. You may laugh. Or even learn something. But being in the audience also means that you are basically . . . sitting. Watching. You are in a passive state. You are witnessing someone else's creative energy. You are being exposed to someone else's imagination and experience.

What about your own imagination? What about your own creativity? Are you making time to express yourself -- your experience, your ideas, your unborn creations?

Let's be honest. It's easier to be in the audience. It's easier to read a book than to write one. It's easier to watch basketball than to play. It's easier to listen to music than to write a song.

Well, why not just create something of your own? Why not just add something to the universe? Today. You might start with a 17 syllable haiku poem. Or maybe a drawing. Or maybe you can start that quilt that has been in your mental incubator for years. Or a song melody that keeps popping into your mind at each traffic light.

Don't pretend that you have no creative capacity. You do. Everyone does. It's just hard to take the first step when you aren't sure what to do or how to do it. Don't let that stop you. And whatever you do, don't pretend that you have no time because there are dirty dishes in your sink. Leave the dirty dishes. Leave the dog's hair on the carpet. Just take ten minutes and do something creative. Something that will wake up your neurons and throw them into a state of chaos. Your neurons need to be shaken up every once in a while. It's good for them. And it's good for you. And it's good for the rest of the world.

Acknowledgments

My father's life was the inspiration for me to write this book, and his death (January, 2014) was the catalyst to publish it sooner, rather than later. Thanks, Dad, for the sad, but important reminder that each human life has an endpoint waiting for us. A special thanks to my Mom for giving me life in the first place. Where would I be without you? There's one woman in my life, Linda, who plays so many roles: my wife, my editor, my colleague, my nutritionist, the mother of my children, ToDo Institute board member and more. She contributed an essay to this book. And proofed it, as well. Thank you, Linda, for sharing this journey with me for the past 26 years.

There are three men who initially developed the methods that are at the foundation of this work. Shoma Morita, M.D. was the founder of Morita Therapy. Ishin Yoshimoto, was the founder of Naikan (self-reflection). And W. Edwards Deming developed Kaizen, a method of continuous improvement for organizations. I am grateful to each of them and to all the karmic forces that made it possible for me to stumble on to their ideas and writings. David Reynolds is primarily responsible for importing Morita's and Yoshimoto's methods into the U.S. and translating their writing into

English. He provided my initial introduction to their work. Thank you, David.

There are a small handful of Buddhist teachers who have had a dramatic influence on my perspective of psychology and spirituality. They are: Pema Chodron, Charlotte Joko Beck, Dzigar Kongtrul, Thich Nhat Hanh, Taitetsu Unno, and, Rev. Kenryu Tsuji, who was my personal teacher for 11 years. Thank you all for expressing your thoughts and wisdom so eloquently in words. And also a deep bow to Eknath Easwaran, a meditation teacher whose writings on mindfulness are some of the most insightful I've ever read.

Several of the contributors to this book are not only colleagues, but dear friends – Margaret, Trudy and Julie – whom I've known for many, many years. And I had the pleasure of working with Kate Manahan during a Naikan retreat years ago. Both my daughters, Chani and Bi, studied Suzuki piano and violin for seven years – a method of music instruction developed by Shinichi Suzuki that captures some of the same values as I've tried to present in this book. I'm honored to have his essay appear in this book. For aspiring authors who find themselves stuck, I highly recommend Steven Pressfield's *The War of Art*. No book does a better job of rousing someone to write. Thank you, Steven.

Nancy Martin was my assistant and the person who helped make this book whole. She is a multitalented, intelligent and caring individual with a wonderful sense of humor. Her presence and support has enriched this book significantly. Thank you.

The person who was "with me" throughout the writing of this book isn't even a person. It's my Golden Retriever, Barley. He gave me an excuse to get up and take a walk when I had been sitting in a chair much too long. It's one of the smartest things any author can do. Thank you, Barley.

This brief page of acknowledgments doesn't really scratch the surface. There are people who lived centuries ago – sages, like Lao Tzu, and haiku poets, like Issa – whose writings deeply touched me. There are objects like my laptop, eyeglasses and coffee cup who traveled with me during early morning writing time. There are forms of energy like electricity and heat that powered my ability to move ideas from thoughts to pages. Remove any one of these and writing a book becomes much more difficult. And finally, there are the donors and members of the ToDo Institute who have made it possible for me to do this work for more than twenty years. I hope this book provides at least a small down payment on the large debt I owe to you all.

About the Author

Gregg **Krech** is one of the leading authorities on Japanese Psychology in North America and is the founding Director of the ToDo Institute, an educational center for purposeful living in Vermont. He is the author of the award-winning book: *Naikan: Gratitude, Grace & the Japanese Art of Self-Reflection* (Stone Bridge Press, 2002), which has been translated into five languages, and the editor of *Thirty Thousand Days: A Journal for Purposeful Living.*

His work has been featured in a wide range of publications including a feature interview in THE SUN magazine, as well as articles in Tricycle, SELF, Utne Reader, Fitness, Counseling Today, Cosmopolitan and Experience Life. Gregg presents to diverse audiences ranging from mental health professionals to Zen practitioners throughout the world. He has been a featured speaker at national conferences on Buddhist Psychology, Mindfulness and Psychotherapy and Attention Deficit Disorder. His other books include *A Natural Approach to Mental Wellness* (ToDo Institute, 2011), and *A Finger Pointing to the Moon* (ToDo Institute, 1996, 2007).

Through his books, distance learning courses and residential retreats Gregg has introduced thousands of people to an approach to life that emphasizes character development over symptom reduction, and continues to point people towards doing something meaningful with their life in spite of their limitations and problems.

Gregg has worked as a volunteer in refugee camps in Thailand, where he worked with orphan children. He now has two beautiful adopted two daughters from China and Vietnam. His personal interests include hiking, piano, haiku poetry, and basketball. He currently lives in residence at the ToDo Institute in Vermont with his wife Linda, daughters Chani and Abbie, and their Golden Retriever, Barley.

You can contact Gregg directly by email with your comments

gregg@todoinstitute.org

and follow his other writing on his blog, Thirty Thousand Days:

www.thirtythousanddays.org

I look for what needs to be done.
After all, that is how the universe invents itself.

- R. Buckminster Fuller

The Art of Taking Action

The Supporting Cast

Assistant Editor

Nancie S. Martin is the author of four non-fiction books, one volume of poetry, and hundreds of magazine and newspaper articles. She has taught adults and children to write more effectively, and has edited numerous national and local publications.

Contributors

Trudy Boyle lives in Ottawa, where she delights in caring for her young grandchildren, writing, photography, cycling and saying YES to family, friends and important matters of the heart. Twice a year, she teaches a program based on Meaningful Life Therapy (MLT) for cancer patients at Wellspring Calgary, where she was formerly the Program Manager.

Linda Anderson Krech, LICSW, is a regular contributor to *Thirty Thousand Days* and author of *Little Dreams Come True*. Prior to her staff role at ToDo, Linda integrated Morita and Naikan into her work within psychiatric rehab programs. Linda has been studying and teaching Japanese Psychology for 25 years.

Jennifer Bucko Lamplough is a Chef Instructor for the Robert Morris University Institute of Culinary Arts in Illinois and is co-author of three American Diabetes Association cookbooks. She has a Certificate in Professional Cooking, a B.A. in Journalism, and an M.B.A. She has appeared as a guest chef on several TV and radio programs. (www.fitfoodiechef.com)

Kate Manahan lives with her husband and their two teenaged sons in Kennebunk, Maine. These days she works as a public school counselor and also gets to host a weekly radio interview program with immigrants and refugees. (www.NewMainersSpeak.com)

Margaret McKenzie is a longtime friend and contributor to the ToDo Institute and former Associate Editor of *Thirty Thousand Days*. She is a social worker and Zen teacher living in the Chicago suburbs. She currently works with individuals and families addressing issues of aging and chronic illness.

Donella Meadows (1941-2001) was a pioneering environmental scientist and writer whose book *The Limits to Growth* (1972) sold millions of copies and was translated into 28 languages. She was a leading voice in the "sustainability movement" and taught at Dartmouth College for 29 years. In 1997, she founded the Sustainability Institute, which included development of an ecological village and organic farm in Hartland Four Corners, Vermont. Reprinted with permission.

Susan Page has been conducting workshops for both singles and couples, nationally and internationally since 1980. She has appeared on the *Oprah Winfrey Show*, *Good Morning America*, CNN, NPR, and radio and TV shows across the country. Excerpts from her works have appeared in many publications. *Why Talking Is Not Enough:8 Loving Actions That Will Transform Your Marriage* © Jossey Bass/John Wiley May 2006. Reprinted with permission.

Stephen Pressfield is the author of *The Legend of Bagger Vance* and historical novels including *Gates of Fire*. His struggles to earn a living as a writer (it took 17 years to get his first paycheck) are detailed in *The War of Art*. His excerpt in this book is from *Do the Work: Overcome Resistance and Get Out of Your Own Way*. Copyright 2011. Reprinted with permission.

Sharon Salzberg is a renowned meditation instructor who has been practicing and studying Buddhism for more than thirty years. She is cofounder of the Insight Meditation Society and the Center for Buddhist Studies in Massachusetts. This essay is reprinted with permission from her book *Faith: Trusting Your Own Deepest Experience* (Riverhead Books, 2002)

Shinichi Suzuki (1898-1998) was the founder of the Suzuki Talent Education method—a method used throughout the world to teach children to play and love music and to cultivate the heart-mind (kokoro) of the individual. From *Nurtured By Love: The Classic Approach to Talent Education*, by Shinichi Suzuki and Translated by Waltraud Suzuki © 1983 by Summy Birchard Inc. Exclusive Print Rights Administered by

Jarno Virtanen lives in Finland. He is on Twitter as @pooljar.

Additional Permissions:

The essay, "Working with the Conditions We Encounter" was adapted from ONENESS, The Quarterly Newsletter of Bright Dawn. **www.brightdawn.org**

If you would like to sign up for our mailing list and receive a

Complimentary Copy of

Thirty Thousand Days: A Journal for Purposeful Living

plus a DISCOUNT CODE

for 25% off an annual subscription

please email
subscriptions@todoinstitute.org with

TTDSUB in the subject line

Thirty Thousand Days is an inspiring (advertisement free) quarterly publication. It is a blend of the practical, the psychological and the spiritual and is the only publication of its kind, exploring the relationship between living well and mental health.

Read a free copy today. We think you'll love it.

www.todoinstitute.org

(802) 453-4440

Made in the USA
Middletown, DE
27 October 2020